Preston Perry is a gift to the church. When we consider the profoundly important work of sharing our faith, we are almost always alluding to one of the most uncomfortable, fear-inducing, and consequently neglected areas of our Christian lives. We need—dare I say, we *depend*—on works like *How to Tell the Truth* to strengthen us where we are most vulnerable. In Preston's story I find my own, and in his perspective my courage increases. Through poetry and passion, clarity and conviction, truth and love—this book is a witness igniter. I am thrilled to see how our mission to evangelize will be set ablaze as a result of this book! Thank you, Preston.

KEVIN "KB" BURGESS
Artist, bestselling author, podcaster

Lies seem to spread faster than the truth. "Fake news" and artificial facts have widened the already broad way. In these pages, Preston Perry has served his generation well by teaching us how to tell the truth, truthfully. Almost biographically, Preston fuels our courage, revisits the essentials, and lights a path back to the narrow road.

DR. CHARLIE DATES
Senior Pastor of Salem Baptist Church of Chicago,
Progressive Baptist Church

T0271456

This book is fantastic. I found myself saying, "Yes, *yes*, YES!" Preston shares his compelling story of becoming a Christian and then provides a road map—through his successes and failures—for how to lovingly and naturally share your faith with others.

SEAN McDOWELL, PhD
Professor of Christian Apologetics at Biola University and author of *A Rebel's Manifesto*

Preston Perry is a bold voice for the gospel. And bold is how we Christians *ought* to speak (Ephesians 6:20). If you're like me, you want to be courageous. But we also want to be gentle, respectful, kind. Preston understands that too. His great new book, *How to Tell the Truth*, can help us grow in sharing the message of Jesus with the beauty of Jesus.

RAY ORTLUND
President of Renewal Ministries, Nashville

Evangelism is a lost art. I don't hear much about evangelism anymore—not from churches, parachurch organizations, and Christians. We need a revival in just sharing our faith. Moreover, we need to be encouraged and taught by people who actually are contagious evangelists. Preston is passionate about evangelism, and his commitment to it is contagious. This work is an accessible tool to aid in all of us . . . taking the communication of the gospel from being left to experts to all believers.

DR. ERIC MASON
Founder and lead pastor of Epiphany Fellowship Church, Philadelphia, PA

PRESTON PERRY
HOW TO TELL
THE TRUTH

THE STORY OF HOW GOD SAVED ME TO WIN

HEARTS—NOT JUST ARGUMENTS

HODDER &
STOUGHTON

First published in Great Britain in 2024 by Hodder & Stoughton Limited
An Hachette UK company

Published in association with Tyndale Elevate, an imprint of
Tyndale House Publishers, Carol Stream, Illinois.

1

A CIP catalogue record for this title is available from the British Library

Trade Paperback ISBN 978 1 399 81902 2

Typeset in Adobe Garamond Pro
Designed by Lindsey Bergsma

Printed and bound in Great Britain by Clays Ltd, Elcograf S.p.A.

Hodder & Stoughton policy is to use papers that are natural, renewable and recyclable
products and made from wood grown in sustainable forests. The logging and manufacturing
processes are expected to conform to the environmental regulations of the country of origin.

Hodder & Stoughton Limited
Carmelite House
50 Victoria Embankment
London EC4Y 0DZ

www.hodderfaith.com

CONTENTS

FOREWORD

HIDE-AND-SEEK IS A GAME CHRISTIANS OUGHT
NOT TO PLAY. Not the version of it taught to us as
children—running into shadows, around corners,
and behind couches with the steady approach of
another child ready to say, "Got you!" The sort of
play I have in mind is the one that begins when
there's a knock at the door. You know something
about the religion of the person who knocked and
the reason they found your home without ever having to twist the knob. Or another version happens
when a friend, a coworker, or a person of another
faith decides to defile your own, making claims
that deny the truth as you know it. These friends
or family have a confidence that might persuade
you to think their views are not all sinking sand.
When intimidated by a Jehovah's Witness's knock
or religious conversations instigated by the scoffers
we know by name, we become children without

faith. Finding a shadow, a corner, or a place to comfort our cowardice, we play an invisible game by hiding ourselves and ultimately the truth we're supposed to tell.

Fear wears many faces. Some of us are afraid to engage the world with the truth of God's gospel because we're afraid of confrontation. There are others who are afraid of what could become of their reputation, peace, and paycheck. Then there are the sincere types who want to speak but don't know what to say, maybe because all they know of the Bible is how it explains that Christ died for the world, and to them, that knowledge doesn't seem good enough. Whatever the cause, fear has to die for dead people to learn how to live.

This may come across as intense, since fear is a constant reality for most of us. So perhaps we need to be reminded of the fear beneath the fear, which is that most of us don't believe God is really with us. That he's sent people into the world to teach others all that he commanded and then left them to fend for themselves. But recall the testimony of the entire Bible. When has God ever sent his people to do anything of eternal value that he did not do *with* them? Whether it's opening the door to "those people," inviting to dinner "that friend," or responding to the articulate lie from "that group," you're not alone in this.

In hide-and-seek, some hide and one seeks. The seeking one's primary goal is to find the hiding ones. It's a version of hunting by which children find joy in "catching" their friends. Some Christians engage the world around them in the same way. Treating the hiding ones—the sinning folk, the unbelieving, and their neighbors of other faiths—as prey instead of people. We've seen this play out in our families, churches, and online, where Christians (or so-called) accurately communicate truth but in such a way that undermines the dignity of those they communicate with.

The love God requires of his saints is not just in the truth telling but in the truth embodying. Which is to say that truth is not just a system of belief that accords with reality as God sees it; truth is a person. To put it simply, if Christ is truth, to be a true truth teller, we need to reflect him as we tell it so that the hiding ones don't just hear the gospel of Christ but see and experience it in the witness of his ambassadors. Embodying truth, love, and compassion cultivates in us a particular wisdom that is often lacking in evangelistic and apologetic resources. It's commonplace for instruction to revolve around the mind of the evangelist and what doctrine they must know for their efforts to be effective. But the success of the evangelist is not solely in the knowing but also in the *being*. God intends for people to love him with all of their heart, mind, and soul, and thus the goal is to engage the entire person in our witness. Not focusing on the mind and missing the heart, or engaging the heart and neglecting the mind. Engaging people is a comprehensive project.

This work in your hands is written by a man who seeks to teach you as best he can how to tell the truth in love. I've seen him do it more times than I can count. There have been countless times when the knock on the door came, the Jehovah's Witness standing behind it then welcomed into our home for a conversation. I've seen him be curious. Prayerful. Discouraged, but then instructed by it. Steadfast in making sure the truth was made plain in his speech and discernible in his body. I've seen him sit in the Scriptures, turning them over in his mind until the living Word became alive in him so that his preaching was an overflow of intimacy as opposed to arrogance. When the woman who worshiped other gods came his way, he discerned that to address her idolatry, he first needed to acknowledge the pain that brought her there. He decided against the usual way, which assumes that all people need is truth and not also a hug. I've also seen him challenge, call out, and confront lies with a boldness that transcended him. I've seen him enter rooms and say things that would've gotten him stoned in another era. And knowing this, he said them anyway.

I say all of this to say, I have seen him time and time again be like Jesus. And that's the whole point of everything, including this work. That you wouldn't hide or even seek but that you would simply *be* like your Lord, full of grace and truth.

Jackie Hill Perry
Bible Teacher,
Author of Holier Than Thou

INTRODUCTION

"Hey. Do you believe in God?"

I've started many conversations with these exact words. I love how a question so simple can take a conversation anywhere. More than that, I love what God can do with a conversation when a heart is committed to sharing his truth with the world around it.

Talking to people about God feeds me in a unique way. It is both a pouring out and a filling up. It requires me to give up some of myself, but at the same time, I don't feel like myself when I *don't* share my faith. I guess what I'm trying to say is, I've accepted that I'm an evangelist at the core. There is a deep burning inside me to share the gospel with those who do not know it.

What is the cause of this burning? Imagine walking around every day of your life, and all you see is people dying of thirst, but you know where they can get free water. In fact, the person who has free water has given *you* access to the water. This is the hard part, though: the people around you don't know that they're dying. They don't even know that they're *thirsty*. Not only do they need you to offer them water, but many of them also need you to prove to them that water is what they need to live. Do you *not* offer the water because you feel like people will reject you? Or do you find ways to show them that they are thirsty and that someone wants to give them a drink?

The latter has called me by name during my time as a Christian. The gospel message is the water the dying world needs. Jesus is the one who has given us access to life, because he has given us access to himself. He is the living well of water that never runs dry. Jesus is the one who wants to quench our thirst forever. If we have the gospel in our possession, why don't we share it with those who need it?

I believe that, as Christians, we are *all* called to share our faith. The reason is that Jesus commanded it:

> All authority in heaven and on earth has been given
> to me. Go therefore and make disciples of all nations,
> baptizing them in the name of the Father and of the
> Son and of the Holy Spirit, teaching them to observe
> all that I have commanded you. And behold, I am with
> you always, to the end of the age.
> MATTHEW 28:18-20

We are *all* called to share our faith, but that looks different for every person. For me, it doesn't matter where—the barbershop, the airport, the grocery store, in the back seat of an Uber ride. There is never really a bad place to talk to someone about the God who created them. You might be different. You might not have a special calling as an evangelist. Sharing the gospel with strangers while in public might not be your thing. And that's okay. God has given each of us different gifts. The key thing is to recognize that God can (and wants to) use you and to be ready when opportunities come.

Here's the thing. While it's true that God has gifted me with a particular type of personality that makes it easier for me to talk to strangers than for some, sharing my faith didn't always come naturally. Many of the things I do are learned skills. I had to work at them. I've also learned quite a bit from the mistakes I've made. And trust me, I've made my share of mistakes while trying to share Jesus with others.

Maybe fear of making mistakes has prevented you from sharing truth with others. In this book we will start a war with those fears. The god of this world wants you to submit to those fears. The devil does not want you to know the evangelist inside you. The devil doesn't want you to know that facing your fears—of looking like you're not knowledgeable, of saying the wrong thing, or of offending someone or being rejected—will help mold you into a better witness for Jesus, if only you would give that fear to God and just go for it.

Maybe you fear that you'll have to defend your faith against those who would attack it. I've seen the word *apologetics* (the term for defending religious doctrine) scare God's saints at times. I think some feel like they have to be a fountain of knowledge or a brilliant scholar to engage in apologetic discourse. But I reject that ideology. Our apologetics and evangelism will always hold hands. As I take you through my own story, I'll explain why I believe we tend to overcomplicate both evangelism and apologetics.

I will also acknowledge that a lot of us have stayed away from apologetics and evangelism because we haven't liked the way we've seen it done. Some Christians hear the word *defend* and lose sight of the fact that the purpose of the defense is to be witnesses and not opponents. YouTube videos with titles like "Christian vs. Muslim" sound more like boxing matches than Christians trying to win hearts. We cannot "make disciples of all nations" if we posture ourselves like enemies.

In fact, that's why I started my YouTube channel where I've shared tips on how to engage people of other faiths with the truth of Jesus and shown some of my own conversations about God with people I've met on the street. I wanted to encourage and equip believers in Jesus to share their faith with boldness, truth, and love.

I've traveled all over the world as a spoken word poet. Seeing the deep, global need for Jesus has made me more invested in the lives of people and has given me a deeper desire to teach and share God's Word. I was fascinated to find that in my time in South Africa, Nigeria, Kenya, London, Sweden, and a host of other places, people around the world have the same questions we have in the United States. Questions like, how do I share the gospel with unbelievers? How do I give truth to my father who is a Jehovah's Witness? What do I say to my brother who is a Hebrew Israelite?

This book is my humble attempt to answer questions like these and share with you how to tell the truth of the gospel—in your context, with the gifts that God has given you, to the people that God has placed in your life. I'll share with you stories from my own life—of my successes and failures—to help you understand how God can use you to reach people with his love and truth. My aim is twofold: to help Christians who don't see themselves as evangelists share their faith where God has placed them, and to correct the combative way we often see evangelism and apologetics done. Sharing our faith is not about winning arguments; it's about winning hearts. And the way we do that is by engaging the world around us with truth, dignity, and respect.

My hope for you as you read this book is to not merely learn a bunch of information but also to learn practical tools for how to apply the information in a way that honors God by honoring people.

Jesus told his disciples that they should be wise as serpents and harmless as doves (see Matthew 10:16). Both doves and serpents are quiet creatures. But notice how often, when we gain knowledge, that can make us very loud.

I believe Jesus is pointing us to a wisdom that creates a quiet calmness with those who do not know him. Jesus told his disciples to be like serpents—cunning and stealthlike—not to do evil like a serpent (we all know about the Garden of Eden) but to do good under people's noses without them even realizing what's happening. He also told his disciples to be harmless as doves, to leave each person better off.

My heart in this book is to help you see that, when we tell the truth of the gospel, what we say is not the only thing that matters—how we tell it holds just as much weight. So keep reading, and learn from my story a better way to tell the truth.

1

UNLIKELY
EVANGELIST

ONE OF THE THINGS I've tried to make clear through my YouTube channel and my speaking about evangelism is that you don't need a theology degree or to know the whole Bible by chapter and verse to tell the truth of the gospel to other people. God uses normal and even unlikely people. Like you. Like me.

While my personality is outgoing, it still surprises me that God would choose to use me to make his glory known. While this book is not a memoir of my life, I want to start the conversation with where I come from—or, should I say, with how God has brought me here. Because if God can use me to win hearts (and not just arguments), he can certainly use you.

My grandmother's home on the far south side of Chicago was a summer haven for me and all my cousins. Chicago was far from a paradise by all accounts, but those summers spent with my cousins at my grandmother's were a delight to me. I think it was the joy of being together.

Picture us, growing up around men standing statue on street corners—neighborhood men shooting dice, hoping to gain a dime for their families. Hustling, struggling, fighting, gambling, but trying. Winning and losing daily.

Our Chicago summers were a tightrope between life and death. My cousins and I dodged bullets while playing in front of loose-jaw fire hydrants sprawling water into our neighborhood. We let those wild mouths loose on the corner while dancing near death like it was normal. It was *our* normal. And so we grew up fearing little, like most people around us.

GOD USES NORMAL AND EVEN UNLIKELY PEOPLE. LIKE YOU. LIKE ME.

The streets of our neighborhood were crowded with different shades of brown boy bodies, hearts all the same shade of courage. When dusk finally grew legs and chased us home, we would head inside to bathe in our grandmother's smile. Her home was a shower and sanctuary of its own. We watched her become a choir, preparing dinner for her thirteen grandsons. We didn't know how privileged we were to sit inside her songs before bed, to grow up planted in her rich soil. We didn't know then how her prayers preserved us for the next day, when evil was walking the streets of our hood, hot with violence, seeking to decompose our melanin.

My cousins and I would sleep on the floor in the basement to be close to one another. I guess that was the only way we knew how to say, "I love you." To say, "These summers we spend together are special." We said those I-love-yous every night by cracking jokes on each other. Nightly conversation and sharing secrets about girls tucked us under the covers. We took turns falling asleep beneath the dim glare of moonlight peeking through the small window above us. I spent many nights before bed soaking in how powerful I felt with my cousins. There I was, preteen Preston, smirking at the threat of death, daring it to come near us tomorrow.

The morning couldn't wake us from our slumber soon enough. In those days, we treated sleep like an inconvenient necessity. Eager for the day, we'd throw our bodies out the front door and lose ourselves in the city too early and unruly for my grandmother's liking. The train ride through each neighborhood was more than a simple daily commute. Watching the window on that floating journey through each neighborhood was a reminder of our placement within the city.

Chicago's south side was intriguingly tragic, a truth that was obvious to us even then. No two days in our neck of the woods were just alike, yet each day was related. Every day saw shoot-outs, fistfights, and police harassment. Living in the city in those days was like being trapped in a broken jukebox, one that refused to play the same song twice and skipped the song you selected, yet everything it played sounded the same.

But the neighborhoods we lived in were much more than bullets and drug transactions. They were filled to the brim with laughter and rich, close-knit communities. The aroma of BBQ often stained the sky around us, keeping us running to somebody's cookout. Radios blasted the soundtrack of my childhood. Ours was a community built generously by decent people. Most of the men in my neighborhood never saw the inside of a college but balanced three or four trades to keep hot food on the table. The dirt caked on their hands was always the complexion of honest work. When we needed something fixed around the house, we didn't look in the phonebook; we called Johnny from down the street. He could repair your hot-water heater and change your car transmission and still make it home in time to tuck his children in bed.

As soon as the summer sun began to head in for the night, elders would come outside to sit on their front porch, drink sweet tea, and fill in crossword puzzles. I always felt like they were watching over us—not the same as angels, but placed there by God to keep us safe all the same.

Back then, I didn't know the sovereign plans of the Lord. I didn't see his hand or face in my mundane. I did, however, see him through my grandmother. Her spirit was still through all the chaos in the city. She would talk to us about God like he was a close childhood friend. She saw the goodness of the Lord everywhere she looked, her joy daily made full and then spilling over into praise shouts and singing throughout the day.

Even though my cousins and I weren't living like we should, she never preached at us or lectured. She just lived her faith out loud and prayed that God would chase us down and catch us before a bullet did.

My grandmother's faith wasn't the only influence on me as I sought to make sense of things. I was such an inquisitive kid: the world around me was a puzzle I got a little closer to solving every day. There was always a question for someone lingering on my tongue. And everybody I saw had a different answer. On Saturdays, 117th Street was a melting pot of people pushing their agendas. The drug dealers tucked into alleyways of city blocks with one eye on a fistful of cash and the other on the undercover police cars threatening to take their freedom. Men of the Nation of Islam and the local Hebrew Israelites each occupied a corner on the main street. Their passion was deafening.

The Hebrew Israelites would yell in every Black ear passing by their side of the sidewalk, "We are a chosen people!" "The so-called Black man is the lost child of Israel!" "The white man has lied to us for years!" They would read from the Bible with big, loud voices so everyone nearby could hear them. After one man would read, another would break down his interpretation of God's Scripture. Their explanations always pointed back to the belief that Black people were the chosen tribe, rather than the God I heard my grandmother sing about. As a result we grew used to their aggression. Very few people would engage them, but whenever someone did, it often escalated to a hostile conversation. The Hebrew Israelites had visceral reactions to being challenged. They would regularly frustrate their challengers with crude jokes and persistent interruptions. Most people passing by would ignore them as a result, but I would always listen to their arguments. I listened for years.

The men of the Nation of Islam were visibly dedicated. Donning heavy suits in the middle of June, they would offer a copy of *The Final Call* newspaper to every passing car with an open window. Their approach was strikingly different from the Hebrew Israelites. They were quiet, graceful, disciplined men. Never forcing their religion down our throats, they politely offered us their literature along with some bean pies for a small fee. For that reason, they were one of the most stable and respected organizations in the neighborhood. They recruited a lot of young men who were searching for hope and spiritual guidance in a community too filled with chaos.

Around midday, the Jehovah's Witnesses would file out of the local Kingdom Hall and rush the front doors of every home in the area with fixed smiles and pamphlets. They were so consistent that there wasn't a house on any street that didn't know when to expect them. Whether people planned to dodge them or welcome them as guests, they knew the Witnesses were coming, and coming with their message.

I realize now that everyone always has a message. Every person in every hood around the world has some kind of belief system they're communicating.

In my summers in Chicago, the belief messengers ranged from the hustlers teaching me to get money; my grandmother telling us to stay out of the streets; some kid trying to come up in his gang with a boastful threat on his lips; and a religious man with a pamphlet and smile.

To all of those people it was no secret the hood was fertile ground. I know now God was using that ground to shape me for the harvest.

As I grew into my teenage years, God was chasing me, although I couldn't see it at the time.

I didn't see it because I was too busy chasing a girl I liked. Her parents had a house church in the apartment complex I lived in. Every Sunday morning, two dozen of the neighborhood's faithful pressed in shoulder to shoulder on well-worn sofas encircling a cluster of tightly packed folding chairs in her family's living room to listen to her father preach, heads nodding and enthusiastic choruses of "amen" yelling back at his fiery sermon.

I was by no means a regular churchgoer, but on this particular morning, the sermon was calling me by name.

I arrived late so I sat in the back, but the pastor's words leaped from the pulpit like a wild beast and began to feast on my conscience. He warned that if we didn't "turn from our sin, repent, and put our hope in Jesus," we would feel God's righteous wrath.

"Every one of us will stand and face God someday," he proclaimed. "Some of us will meet him as a friend, others as a judge. And if you think God being love means that he won't destroy everything he hates, you don't understand what love is!"

That shook me. I had heard preachers talk about God before, but never like this. It was the first time I had ever understood that I was a sinner and that God had a beef with the way I was living my life.

Even so, I did not turn to Jesus that morning. But from that day forward, I was keenly aware that God was watching me.

Watching me break into people's homes to steal things that did not belong to me.

Watching me smoke weed and sell drugs.

Watching me fight and fornicate and get kicked out of school again and again and again.

Watching me do all kinds of crazy, immoral, sinful things. I knew God was mad at me. But I also knew that saying yes to him meant saying no to all the sin I loved that never loved me back.

It was a warm spring day. The hum of morning was quiet, like all the mornings that came before it. While still in bed, I heard gunshots echo in the distance.

Who's shooting this early in the morning?

I heard gunshots a second time, and this time they sounded closer. I stuck my head out my window. There was my friend Chris, running from between two apartment buildings down the street from my house. Running like death was behind him. His eyes were wide, and terror clung to his cheeks. Five seconds later, a man I didn't know appeared, running from the same direction, hugging a pistol with his fist and shooting at my friend like he was on a mission. Those shots forced him to the ground.

I raced downstairs, calling to my mom as I passed the

kitchen, "Somebody just shot Chris!" My frantic cry was only outdone by my friend Slim, who was closer to Chris. When I reached Chris, Slim and our other friend Hollywood were already lifting him off the ground to carry him closer to Slim's house.

The three of us hovered over him, helpless as he cried, "Don't let me die! Don't let me die!" over and over as blood was a waterfall near his collarbone. Hollywood took off his shirt and pressed it firmly against the bleeding.

"What do we do, man? What do we do?!" Slim yelled and looked in my eyes for an answer. He saw none.

"We need to get him to the hospital," Hollywood said, looping his arms under Chris's and lifting him into a sitting position.

"Boys!" My mom raced into the street in her robe and slippers, a big bath towel in hand. "Don't move him! You don't know where the bullet is!" There are some things a mother shouldn't know—like how a hollow-tip bullet is designed to decorate someone's insides. A regular bullet goes straight through the body, but a hollow-tip bullet is creative. Once it enters the body, it does to the flesh what it wants. Once it's in, you never know the damage it has done just by looking at the outside. "Just lay him back down," she directed us. "I called 911. They're on their way." Then, like it was second nature, she knelt down and tended to the bleeding.

"Don't let me die. Don't let me die." Chris's eyes couldn't stay still. They looked like frantic birds flying in the dusk with no vision. His voice grew softer, like the last line in a sad song.

"Shhhh . . . don't talk, baby." My mom rubbed her soft

words into his wounds to soothe his mind. "It's gonna be okay. Help is coming."

I watched helplessly. I tried to hold the back of his head still, but my hand had a mind of its own. It kept shaking without my permission. Blood seemed to be coming from everywhere, soaking into the pavement, my shorts, my T-shirt—a red river of life leaving my friend right in front of me.

"Preston." Slim pulled me from the red sea back to the shores. "Man, you gotta pray for him."

I froze. In my mind, I was about as far from God as you could get. Mostly I just regurgitated stuff I had heard my grandmother say, but to guys like Slim and Hollywood, I sounded spiritually mature.

"Yeah, bruh . . . pray for him, Preston," Hollywood pleaded. I can still remember how desperate they sounded. At that moment it felt like my hypocrisy was on full display. I couldn't pretend I knew the Lord in a time like this.

I looked down at Chris, new tears escaping his eyes and running across his old tear marks the color of white ghosts, my mom pressing her now blood-soaked towel against his collarbone where the bleeding seemed to be heaviest. *Hollow-tip bullets.* One of them had come in through his upper back and violently bloomed open like a flower in early May, tearing up muscle, soft tissue, and arteries as it moved through the body, looking for a way out.

"Please, don't let me die."

I opened my mouth to speak, but my conscience stopped the words in my throat. Who was I to ask God for help? I was an enemy of God, just like Chris. Chris's blood that baptized my clothes that morning could just as easily have been my own. Why would God listen to me?

"Hold on, bro." I reached into my back pocket and grabbed my phone. *Please be home.* "Mrs. Collier?" Mrs. Collier was my ex's mom and a pastor. I knew God would listen to her. "Yeah, it's Preston. I'm here with Chris. He's been shot, and it's really bad. Can you please pray for him?"

She asked me to put the phone to his ear. I leaned in and listened as she led him through the Sinner's Prayer. "Chris," she said, "you need to ask the Lord to forgive you for your sins."

I closed my eyes tight. *Listen to her, bro.* A siren called out for Chris in the distance.

"Do you hear me?" she asked. "You need to ask God to forgive you for your sins." She might as well have been talking to me.

"*I don't want to die. I don't want to die.*" By this time, Chris's voice was a whisper.

"Preston, I need you to hold this right here," my mom said, nodding at the crimson-stained towel pressed against Chris's collarbone. "He's bleeding out. I need to get another towel."

Mrs. Collier just kept repeating, "Ask the Lord to forgive you."

"*I don't want to die.*"

"Preston!" my mom all but shouted. "Do you hear me?" All I could hear were Mrs. Collier's words echoing in my head.

"Ask the Lord to forgive you."

"Preston!"

"Ask the Lord to forgive you."

I don't want to die.

I don't want to die.
We don't always get what we want.
Chris's life ended that day on the way to the hospital.
Mine was just getting started.

Chris's death was a wake-up call. I knew I had to change the way I was living. That was hard to do when all my friends were criminals. Later that week, I called my aunt Denise. She was a pastor at a church out in Olympia Fields, a suburb roughly twenty miles south of Chicago, and she agreed to let me stay with her for a while. There was just one catch.

"If you're going to live in this house," she said, "you need to go to church." Man, looking back, if I didn't know any better, I'd have sworn that God was setting me up.

My aunt was a righteous woman. She stood five-foot-nothing, but her smile was much bigger than this world. She reminded me of my grandmother. The songs she sang in the morning carried my heart the same way my grandmother's did. She lived out her faith so loud. She was a leader and great Bible teacher in public, but I saw what happened in private, and that was good for a young soul like mine, a soul that was searching for God in a world filled with lies and many voices trying to earn my worship.

My aunt Denise opened the doors of her home to me at a time when there weren't a lot of doors for me to walk through. There weren't many options for a young man like myself, with no vision of what he wanted to be or do in life. But Aunt Denise

MAN, LOOKING BACK, IF I DIDN'T KNOW ANY BETTER, I'D HAVE SWORN THAT GOD WAS SETTING ME UP.

invited me into a stable life and a place I could call home. She helped me enroll in a vocational college. She didn't know what I was called to do in life either, but she knew I needed structure. Her being in my life gave me just that.

But more than that, she played an instrumental role in my salvation.

For the first couple of weeks that I lived with her, I would wake up in the morning, only to find an oily substance on my forehead. There were mornings I would brush my teeth and my eyes would catch a glimpse of my shining forehead in the mirror. I was so confused. For a while only heaven knew why I looked like someone had rubbed a piece of fried chicken across my face while I was sleeping.

Then one morning it all made sense.

It was around 5:00 a.m. I was usually asleep, but on this morning, my body was only a shallow grave of rest. So when someone touched my head, I woke up in wonder and confusion. My eyes cracked open to find my aunt standing over me with a bottle of oil in her hands, her face fixed in a subtle cry. Feeling awkward at her presence, I closed my eyes just as quickly as I had opened them. I kept quiet and lay as still as an ocean trying not to wake the waves. I waited to see why she was in my room.

She touched my forehead again, this time with oil slick on her fingers. She began praying for me.

"Save his soul, Lord."

"Watch his coming in and going out."

"Keep him, Lord."

"In your wrath, remember mercy, O God."

"Reveal yourself to him."

"Make yourself known in his heart."

These were some of the prayers she uttered in a quiet moan, tears running frantic down her face. Her prayers sounded like she was begging God on my behalf, desperation clinging to her every word in such a precious yet careful way, like a poor man holding brittle gold between his tired fingers. I could feel her love for God and for me traveling through my body, as if her prayer was God's way of depositing his mercy inside a soul that did not know him yet.

My body was fully awake now. God was preparing me for the awakening of my soul.

A couple mornings later, over breakfast, Aunt Denise announced, "I've asked a young man to stop by and talk with you today. I think you'll really like him. He's taking classes over at Moody."

My shoulders slumped. I turned my head away so she wouldn't see how unexcited I was to meet him. I knew what people from Moody were like, and I didn't need a starched-shirt, Billy Graham wannabe preaching at me all afternoon.

Two hours later, my aunt and I were sitting on her porch when the dude pulled into the driveway in a Mustang. I was unsettled as I waited for him to get out of his car. Even though his car was tight, I just knew I was about to see a typical churchgoer, the kind of person that had judged me my whole life. But I was surprised. His baggy jeans looked like they hadn't had a day off in a while, yet he was fashionable all the same. He was wearing Jordan sneakers—but not the Team Jordans the uncool kids wore in high school. These were the hard-to-get kind we waited outside Foot Locker to get on Saturday mornings. He had on a Bulls cap I immediately wanted for myself and a black hoodie. His appearance grabbed my attention. I thought, *This dude don't look like no Christian. He look like a hood cat.* He walked up to me smiling wide, and his smile didn't seem fake. He looked like he was genuinely excited to meet me. He stuck his fist out. "What's up, brother? I'm Gary."

"'Sup, man," I said. "I'm Preston." We shook hands. In the Black community, a handshake is the first way to feel if a person has anything in common with you. It can determine if you're going to entertain a conversation or quickly look for a way out. Gary shook my hand like all the people I grew up with did.

And the dude just kept smiling. "Yeah, your aunt told me about you. Man"—he shook his head—"you living with a mighty woman of God. She prayed for me many times, bro."

"I heard you go to Moody, so her prayers must've worked," I joked. We both laughed.

Then he shifted gears. "Hey, you hoop?"

I nodded. "Oh, fo sho, I hoop."

"Cool. I was gonna head over to Washington Park, see if I can get a pickup game going. You wanna come?"

Washington Park? That was a rough neighborhood. *This*

dude's gonna drive a Mustang into that neighborhood, and he's not from there? This dude trying to get us robbed?

"You sure?" I asked. "You know it's wild over there, right?"

His smile curled confidently. "We good, bro. I know a lot of guys over there. I hoop over there all the time."

On the way into the city, Gary told me a little about himself. Turns out he was a former gang member and dealer who grew up in one of the worst neighborhoods in Chicago. His dad was a pastor, but Gary didn't go to church very often. In fact, his father had made him choose, either the streets or the church. Gary chose the street life, but he gave it up when God breathed new life inside him.

Man, the dude was practically me! There was just one difference.

"Where you at with the Lord?" he asked as we turned off the expressway.

"Me and the Lord?" I thought about it for a second. "Yeah . . . we good." I couldn't tell if he believed me or not, probably because I didn't believe myself. To his credit, Gary didn't push it. He just said, "Cool, cool" and left it at that.

When we got to Washington Park, Gary walked right over to a bunch of guys who were hooping on the basketball court. As we approached them, Gary stretched his smile so wide they wouldn't see us as a threat. "What's up, brothas! My name's Gary. This is Preston. Y'all mind if we play with y'all?" At first they said nothing but stared at us for what felt like an eternity. Finally, they broke the silence. "Yeah, we're playing a game of 21. Y'all can jump in."

Gary clapped his hands together. "Cool, cool." And then we just started playing.

Gary was good about that, as I came to find out. He could start a conversation with anybody, and he would always build some type of rapport. And then after we'd finished playing, Gary would share his faith. He would be like, "Oh, man, I enjoy playing with y'all brothers. It was a joy." Then he'd follow up with something like "This might seem weird, but can I pray with y'all? There's a lot of stuff going on. Young brothers out here dying. Y'all mind if we pray?" And they would always say yes. What else could they say? We would gather, grab hands on the basketball court, and pray. The first time we did that, I was thinking, *This dude is crazy. We're in Washington Park, and he's asking these street dudes to pray with him?*

And he *would* pray—a sincere prayer. And after almost every time he would pray, it would lead to a conversation.

He would always share his story about being a member of a Chicago gang and how Jesus saved him. But before he could lose their attention, he'd say, "I'm not trying to preach at y'all. This is just what God did with my life. I met Jesus one day, and I never was the same."

Everything Gary did was fascinating to me. He was just a normal dude from Chicago. There wasn't any phoniness to him—no pretense—and that was refreshing.

And as I hung out with Gary, I stopped doing a lot of the stuff I had been doing. I had started to mimic his life. I think because my life mimicked Gary's, I started to convince myself that we had matching hearts, that I was on fire for the Lord like he was. But my heart wasn't new. I wasn't a Christian. Yet.

My heart was not yet born again, and the day that became painfully obvious to me will forever sit in the corner of my mind.

It was Thursday afternoon. The sun was shining something crazy, its rays spilling over the shoulders of Chicago, giving life to the battered body of the city. Gary came to pick me up to play basketball in Washington Park. As I had learned, Gary would intentionally go to the most violent neighborhoods to hoop so he could share the gospel with the guys on the court afterwards.

Before we headed to the basketball court, Gary had to go to the bank. We pulled into the drive-thru. The teller was a beautiful cinnamon brown girl, her curled hair a pretty, silky sand color with streaks of black. From my view in the passenger seat, I saw her eyes grab Gary and hold him closely, as if she wanted to dance or to hear the way his heart beat inside his chest. While asking for his ID, her smile was saying, *Talk to me—I know your name, but I want you to know mine.*

Gary appeased her. He awkwardly asked, "How's your day going?"

"It's going better, now that I've seen you," she replied.

Gary laughed, put his head down, and smiled into his lap so she wouldn't see the blushing forest fire she ignited on his face. I sat there quietly, my ears an open gate as she continued to flirt and engage Gary with small talk. I just knew this exchange would end with him getting her number or him asking her out.

Surprisingly, it didn't.

As soon as the transaction was over, Gary ended the conversation abruptly, told her to have a nice day, and sped off. I took a quick glance at the young lady's face as we drove away, and she looked perplexed. I was confused as well, and secretly shaming Gary in my heart. I thought he was crazy for not taking such a beautiful woman up on her advances when she had so neatly gift wrapped all of her attention for him.

For the next ten minutes Gary drove in silence, his face soaking in deep thought as he stared intently out the window. I assumed he was kicking himself for letting such a beautiful woman get away.

Gary pulled the car over to the side of the road. "P," he said, "I want to apologize to you, man."

My face curled into a question mark. "Why are you apologizing to me?"

"I was not a good example to you back at the bank when I was talking to that girl," Gary replied, his face joyless and empty, like an abandoned church on Sunday.

I was still puzzled. "But she was flirting with you," I said. "What did you do wrong?"

"I know, I know," Gary replied, "but my heart wasn't right, Preston. For a while now that girl has been flirting with me, and that time I entertained it, and what makes it worse is that you were in the car to witness it! I have no desire to pursue her, and all my thoughts were lustful when we were talking. I'm so convicted, bro. Could you pray with me?"

I was still a little confused, but I said, "Yeah, sure, Gary, let's pray." I was amazed as Gary began talking to the Lord, asking him for his forgiveness. His prayer was so sincere. He spoke to God like he was a good friend that Gary had just let down. As Gary prayed, my mind raced. His prayer faded into the background as the thoughts in my head got louder. At first, I tried to tell myself that he was overreacting. Then I thought, *Well, maybe he's just being dramatic like all the other church folk.* But Gary was unlike any other churchgoer I had ever met. *Nah, that can't be it.* Here he was, a few years older but a young man like myself, that lived out his convictions when no one else was watching to praise him for it.

I had never seen a young man flee lust like every woman not named "Wife" was made of flames. I couldn't deny that this moment was pure and genuine. And just like that, a light came on for me. A hard truth came to my mind as if someone else had placed it there: *This is what it means to truly love God, and I don't love him like Gary loves him.* That day Gary's life showed me that I was a cemetery, dead inside.

I wanted what Gary had. I just had to find out how to get it.

After what happened with Gary, the rest of the week I had been confronted with the weight of my sin. And now, it was too much for my weary soul to carry.

That's the interesting thing about sin. You can live comfortably with it all your life, but once you are made aware of how offensive it is to a holy and righteous God, it becomes a nagging, unwanted guest in the home of your heart.

There was a problem, though. I didn't know what repentance looked like. I couldn't remember the words of the prayer Mrs. Collier said to Chris that day as he lay dying in the street. I didn't even know if I should say that prayer at all. All I knew was I didn't know God, and that weighed heavy on my heart.

I got up and walked back and forth between my bed and the window, searching for the right language to talk to God. Initially, I just wanted to ask for his forgiveness, but the words couldn't find my mouth in the new morning light.

I began to cry like my heart was broken, because it was. For a while now I felt like God was calling me to himself, and at the moment, I was ready to surrender, but I couldn't find the right words to say. What I know now that I didn't know then is that God didn't need my words; he was listening to my heart. In fact, he had been talking to my heart the whole morning. I cried for an hour straight.

By this time, the sun had swallowed dusk whole and overtaken my bedroom, and the flood of tears finally stopped. I walked over to the mirror that hung over my dresser next to my Tupac and DMX posters to look my reflection in the eyes. I wondered if I would see the same shame I felt in my heart. All I saw was a broken man. I didn't know if that was good or bad. My eyes were swollen with grief. The dried tear marks on my face looked like a road map to freedom, but I still didn't know the way. I just knew I wanted to love God how I saw my grandmother and Aunt Denise and Gary love him.

I cried again. I was frustrated by all the crying, but it was a purging of sorts. I began to think of all the bad things I'd done that deserved death and started uttering words. "I'm sorry, God, forgive me. I'm sorry, God, forgive me." At that moment, a sweet presence wrapped me blanketlike. My heart felt a soothing warmth, similar to how the skin feels when the sun greets the body after a cold swim.

I cried out and said, "Lord, I want to love you like Gary loves you." I can still smell that moment. I can still taste it. It was the greatest moment of my life. In that moment my heart was saying, "Here, God, take it. Here, God, I'll take you instead of battered shame and overwhelming grief." I knelt by my bed and thanked God for the freedom I felt. I thanked him over and over until I grew tired and lay prostrate on my wilted bedroom carpet. A sweet hush fell on my room, like a mother nursing a new life to sleep. A quiet entered my body and set up in my bones. A stillness rested deep in my marrow. I had not yet known this feeling, but I knew that this was peace. God had officially taken my heart out of the concrete jungle and invited me into a garden—a garden where death was absent but life was present and all around me. There my heart was calm, but my body was so tired. I passed out right where my body lay on the floor, and it was the best sleep I've ever had.

When I awoke around noon, my body still felt like it had taken a beating, but my soul felt new. It felt like somebody came and cleaned up all the mess that was inside me, and now my heart could live comfortable inside my body. The only thing I could think about was the goodness of God—how he had chased me for years until he finally had me. How he wanted me when I didn't want him. I knew now that I loved him.

That morning was historic for me. It was the morning that God saved my soul.

And from that moment on, I started sharing my faith with whoever would listen.

As I look back over my own story, I am again struck not just by how God could rescue me, but by how he could *use* me to reach others.

The apostle Paul felt the same way. Learning about Paul was an encouragement for me because I saw myself in his God-breathed story. I, too, had a brick for a heart that I often stoned Christians with, but like Paul, I met Jesus one day, and now I love him with all that I am. I wasn't always a saint drenched in hymns in the morning. I was once a rebellious black sky running from the Son. Paul was the same. But after Jesus met Paul on the way to Damascus to bring him into the morning, Paul never forgot the darkness of night that God had brought him from. Paul never lost his sense of awe that God could use him. And shouldn't this be the testimony of everybody that God has brought out of darkness and into his marvelous light?

Paul's ability to remember where God brought him from helped him to abandon pride and adopt gratefulness on his journey with Jesus. He wrote to his young protégé Timothy, "The saying is trustworthy and deserving of full acceptance, that Christ Jesus came into the world to save sinners, of whom I am the foremost" (1 Timothy 1:15). Even when Paul was traveling the world and telling people about Jesus, he remembered where he came from and what it meant for him—a former enemy of God—to be God's messenger.

Maybe you're reading this book and you're from the hood like me. Maybe you're from a place where seminary is not the first option for many. Maybe you're a stay-at-home mom balancing bills and diapers while trying to study God's Word during naptime. Maybe you're an HBCU student, and hearing that Christianity is "the white man's religion" is a new and confusing experience for you. Whoever you are, my prayer is that you would not feel like you are disqualified to share this treasure we call the gospel with the world. If you are no longer in darkness, that means you can see clearly. That's what qualifies you to be an evangelist.

God isn't seeking to use special people. He just wants to use us—normal people—to show the world that we were once blind, but now we can see, and they could too if only they would repent and believe. God doesn't use us *because* of ourselves. God uses us *in spite of* ourselves. Paul writes,

> Consider your calling, brothers: not many of you
> were wise according to worldly standards, not many
> were powerful, not many were of noble birth. But
> God chose what is foolish in the world to shame the
> wise; God chose what is weak in the world to shame

the strong; God chose what is low and despised in the world, even things that are not, to bring to nothing things that are, so that no human being might boast in the presence of God.

I CORINTHIANS 1:26-29

Paul makes it clear to the church in Corinth that God didn't choose them because they were wealthy, influential, talented, or smart. God has his own purposes, and he delights in using our weaknesses to display his glory. As Paul writes in another letter to this church, "We have this treasure [specifically, the gospel message] in jars of clay, to show that the surpassing power belongs to God and not to us" (2 Corinthians 4:7).

When Jesus gave the great commission to his disciples, he didn't tell them, "Therefore, go and make disciples of all nations . . . but first, get a degree in biblical exegesis and another in apologetics, and then spend another several years in seminary." Those things are valuable, and thank God he has equipped his church with people who have done that necessary work. But those things don't automatically make us effective in God's Kingdom. Jesus ends by telling them that he will be with us until the end of the age. Jesus tells us to go and make disciples because the *Holy Spirit* will empower us to do it. Jesus, in his last words to his disciples before he was taken into heaven, told them, "You will receive power when the Holy Spirit comes upon you, and you will be my witnesses in Jerusalem and in all Judea and Samaria, and to the end of the earth" (Acts 1:8). The Holy Spirit empowers the witness.

The Holy Spirit is the great equalizer when it comes to evangelism. God did not give us his Spirit merely so we can study and pour into people what we know. He gave us his Spirit so he can speak through us. I'm not knocking knowledge by any means. The knowledge we have of God is essential to our faith, and God's Word tells us his people perish for lack of it (see Hosea 4:6). But what if it's possible for us to trust so much in what we know that we become insensitive to what the Holy Spirit wants us to say? Jesus told his disciples that when they were brought before powerful people to answer for their faith, they should "not be anxious how you are to speak or what you are to say, for what you are to say will be given to you in that hour. For it is not you who speak, but the Spirit of your Father speaking through you" (Matthew 10:19-20).

We see the truth of this over and over again in the book of Acts. On the day of Pentecost, the Holy Spirit fell heavy on the church in Jerusalem, and they were given the power to preach—and three thousand people were saved. In Acts 4, when Peter and John were brought before the Jewish leaders to answer for healing a man who was crippled, they gave a bold defense of their faith in Jesus. And what astonished the Jewish leaders was that they "perceived that [Peter and John] were uneducated, common men.... And they recognized that they had been with Jesus" (Acts 4:13).

You don't have to be Billy Graham or even Gary or me to be bold in sharing your faith. You just need to be with Jesus. While in his company, he'll make us like him if only we ask.

One thing about this last point: context matters when it comes to evangelism. No offense to the Christians that came before Gary, but their lives weren't as effective with me as Gary's was. And that's because representation matters, especially when it comes to seeing someone live holy. I needed to see that God calls people like me too. People need to see what it's like for God to change a life—they need to see a before and after that they can understand. It's hard to imagine our lives being a certain way if nobody that looks like us lives this way. God used Gary to help me hope for a new soul of my own. If all I saw were people who grew up in church living their lives for Jesus, I might think, *You grew up in church. Of course you're a Christian.* But to see someone who used to sell drugs and be a gang member serve the Lord was monumental for me. Gary's story mirroring my own made his relationship with God feel more tangible, like if God met him one day, maybe he died to meet me too.

And here's the thing: you can be that person for someone else. They don't need a famous person to convert to Christianity or tell them about Jesus to see that living for him is possible. They need to see *you*, in whatever your context is, living your life for Jesus, making belief in him seem possible. Desirable.

REPRESENTATION MATTERS, I NEEDED TO SEE THAT GOD CALLS PEOPLE LIKE ME.

Jesus gave the great commission as a command to *all* his disciples, because all of his disciples, through the power of the Holy Spirit, can do it.

Now that you know my story and have seen how God can use you—where you are, within your unique context—let's look at some tools to make you more effective in telling the truth of the gospel to a world that needs to hear.

2

ACCIDENTAL
APOLOGIST

I WAS IN MY SECOND SEMESTER at the two-year vocational college my aunt Denise had enrolled me in, beard freshly grown and a world away from the life of sin God called me out of. But my aunt said I lacked direction. She wasn't wrong. I had no idea what I wanted to do. All I knew was that I loved art, I loved rap, and I loved poetry. But my aunt was like "Preston, how are you going to make a living writing poetry? You need to learn a trade." The funny thing was, I would eventually make a living from writing poetry. But God had a few plans for me first. Before I made a living as a welder of words, I found myself in a classroom at Prairie State College learning how to be a more traditional welder of metal.

I know, right?

One day this guy walked into class wearing perfectly pressed khakis, a polo shirt, and fancy black dress shoes—you know, one of those job interview type outfits—and made his way to the seat in front of me. I noticed he had been carrying a Bible, so I asked him, "Are you a Christian, bro?"

He sized me up for a second, smiled, and said, "Yeah . . ."

"That's dope, bruh. Me too." I stuck my hand out. "I'm Preston."

"John," he said, shaking my hand.

To be honest, if he hadn't been carrying a Bible, I probably wouldn't have talked to him at all. He didn't look like the kind of guy I usually hung out with. I was just excited to find another Christian at that school.

"Yeah, man." I lifted up my English Standard Version Bible proudly to show him we're on the same side of this spiritual war. "I love the Bible. What are you reading right now?"

I expected him to say something like "I'm studying the Psalms" or "I'm working my way through Romans," but instead, he launched into a speech about how he was reading along with his church family on how Jehovah is coming back to save the world from corruption and pain.

Because of Gary's and my aunt Denise's leadership, I was used to reading the Bible for myself, so I thought it was odd that he had a Bible in hand and responded with what his church was studying and didn't tell me what *he* was reading. But I also believed Jehovah would return one day, so I said amen and asked him what church he went to.

"I go to Kingdom Hall," he said.

I'd never heard of it. Then he asked me, "How did you become a Christian?"

Because class was going to start in a couple minutes, I didn't give him my full testimony. I just told him that a friend of mine had walked with me and taught me all about Jesus and what it meant to be saved.

"Well, how do you know everything your friend taught you is right?"

"What do you mean?" I asked.

He leaned in, like he had a secret to share and didn't want the rest of the class to hear. "I hate to tell you this, but the church has been teaching you a lot of the wrong things." He said it with his chest swollen with authority and his face creased with concern. I'm pretty sure my facial expression was saying, *Bruh, you don't even know what church I go to.* Suddenly this dude seemed to act much older than he appeared. He reminded me of the old church deacons who used to stare me down when we would go to church. They were always so serious, so I would just keep my distance. But this guy was near and apparently needed answers from me.

I leaned back in my seat and crossed my arms, suddenly feeling defensive but giving him time to explain himself. "How so?" I said.

"Well, for one thing," he said matter-of-factly, "Jehovah's name has been taken out of your Bible thousands of times."

"What do you mean, Jehovah's been taken out of my Bible?" I flipped my Bible open and pointed to one of my favorite passages, John 3:16-17. "Look—right here it says, 'For God so loved the world, that he gave his only Son, that whoever believes in him should not perish but have eternal life. For God did not send his Son into the world to condemn the world, but in order that the world might be saved through him.'"

"Like I said"—he smirked, setting his stuff down on his desk—"Jehovah's name has been taken out."

"Yeah," I started, "I know Jehovah is one of God's names, but—"

"Jehovah," he said, cutting me off, "is the name above every name."

"Aw, see, that's where you're wrong, bro," I corrected him. "*Jesus* is the name above every name. Look . . ." I flipped over to Philippians, turned my Bible towards him, and pointed to 2:9. "It says right here: 'Therefore God has highly exalted him and bestowed on him the name that is above every name.'"

John leaned back in his seat and looked at me like I was covered in blasphemy. "So you believe Jesus is greater than Jehovah?"

"No, I believe Jesus *is* Jehovah."

He pointed at me, smiled, and said, "*That's* what you've been taught wrong."

I was so confused. The dude said he was a Christian, so why was he arguing with me about who Jesus is?

By this point I felt like I was on trial. So I looked at him like I was a defense attorney and said, "You said you're a Christian, right?"

"Actually," he said calmly, "I'm one of the true Christ followers on earth."

I leaned my head to the side, twisted my lips in a knot so something offensive wouldn't fly out of my mouth, and blinked my eyes quickly like hazard lights so he would know I thought something is really wrong here. "What is a true Christ follower?" I asked.

"True Christ followers *honor* Jesus and *respect* Jesus, but we don't *worship* Jesus."

"Oh, nah, bro, you off. You *way* off!" I said. "Jesus is the way, the truth, and the life." It was at this point that a small crowd started to form around us.

"Well, let me ask you this," he said, flipping over to Matthew 24 and turning the Bible back towards me. "It says right here that Jesus doesn't know the day or the hour that God will come back for his people. So if Jesus is God, why is he limited in knowledge?"

Like mice looking for the last grains of rice in the kitchen, my mind scattered, searching for an answer . . . but I couldn't find one. I stared at him blankly. My mind was playing tug-of-war between confusion and irritation.

Then he flipped back to Philippians. "And look, it says right here that Jesus humbled himself and made himself obedient to the Father. If he's obedient to the Father, how can he be equal to the Father?"

I didn't have any response for that one either.

He just kept going. "And let me ask you this. Who was Jesus praying to in the garden? Was he praying to himself?"

"No!" I said it quickly before he could smack me with another question. "He was praying to his Father."

"But you said Jesus and God are the same person."

"No, he's not the same person," I tried to clarify, "but they're both God."

"So they're two gods?"

"No, they're not two gods." Dude had me rattled! "It's like . . . the Trinity is not two gods . . ." I was so flustered I could barely think straight.

"So the Trinity is one guy *and* three guys?" He covered his eyes sarcastically with his hand and laughed at me like I was a child. "Bro, that doesn't make any sense." I *felt* like a little child. But the truth is I was much younger in my faith. I was only a baby.

Before I could respond, my friend Brittany, who had been listening in, leapt to my defense. "Listen," she said, with all the attitude she could muster, "I don't know who you are, but Preston knows what he's talking about."

Did I, though? I knew in my heart that what I believed was true. I believed that God saved me, and I believed that the Lord revealed to me who he was. And yet I didn't know how to defend what I believed. I couldn't explain how the triune God of Scripture existed. It was humbling. Actually, it was humiliating. I mean, I was "Preston the evangelist" at this school, and all of a sudden, I couldn't even

> I KNEW IN MY HEART THAT WHAT I BELIEVED WAS TRUE. AND YET I DIDN'T KNOW HOW TO DEFEND WHAT I BELIEVED.

explain who Jesus is! The whole time my heart felt like it was trying to escape my chest. It was beating like John was trying to steal my faith from me. Everybody was staring at me, waiting for me to respond. I had to say something, so I blurted out the only thing I could think of. "I just know that Jesus is Lord."

"That doesn't make him God, though," John said and smirked. A few people snickered.

"Bro, what religion are you?"

He smiled calmly. "I'm a Jehovah's Witness." All the lights in my head turned on. *You mean to tell me I was talking to a Jehovah's Witness the whole time?*

By the grace of God, the instructor walked in, and John turned around in his seat. I flipped my Bible shut in frustration.

All this time I had thought I was some spiritual giant, telling everyone I could about Jesus, and then this dude walked up in his freshly pressed khakis talking about "Jehovah" and quickly folded my argument up and put it in his back pocket. I sat there, hot. I mean, I was a furnace, ready to burn him with a fist of fury. Yeah, I can't even front—my flesh wanted to fight. My old self was buried that day in my room when Jesus called the grave out of me, but this was the first time he came back from the dead, fuming. I sat there quiet for the remainder of the class, embarrassed and angry.

I knew what John was saying about Jesus was wrong, but I couldn't find the words to explain why. I mean, I knew the gospel message, but apart from a handful of verses that I'd committed to memory, I really hadn't studied Scripture very much. The only thing I knew for sure was that the story about a Messiah who came to dwell in human history and rescue sinners was true. I needed help, and I knew who to call.

"Aw, bro, you got into an apologetics argument."

"What's apologetics?" I asked. I'd never heard Gary use that word before. I assumed it had something to do with apologizing, but the only thing I felt sorry about was that I couldn't answer any of John's questions.

"It's basically a defense of religious doctrine," he explained. When I didn't say anything, he added, "It means to defend your faith."

"John said he was a Jehovah's Witness," I said, "but he also told me he was a Christian." Then I remembered. "He also said he was a true Christ follower. Man, what's that supposed to mean?"

"Yeah . . ." Gary began. I could just picture him sitting back in his chair, smiling. "They say that, but Jehovah's Witnesses aren't really Christians." Then Gary started telling me about what Jehovah's Witnesses believe—that they don't believe in hell, they believe only 144,000 people will make it into heaven, and they think Jesus just started ruling in heaven in 1914.

"Bro, that's crazy," I blurted.

"They base a lot of their beliefs on stuff in Revelation and on their own unique interpretation of Scripture," Gary said. "Let me guess . . . did he bring up Philippians 2:8? Or ask who Jesus was praying to in the garden?"

"Man, he did ask about the garden and Philippians!" I said, stunned. "How'd you know that?"

"Listen, bro," he laughed, "I've talked to these guys more times than I can count. They're well trained in Scripture. Their theology is off, but they're well trained."

I felt so disappointed that I couldn't seem to find the words to defend my faith.

"Don't sweat it, P," Gary reassured me. "Dude caught you off guard is all. A lot of the stuff Jehovah's Witnesses believe sounds almost identical to Christianity. That's probably why he didn't tell you he was a Witness right up front. He wanted to test you—see how much you knew, see if he could trip you up and get you to question what you believe."

Gary walked me through some of the things that seemed off in my encounter with John, and I realized that if I was going to talk to John about *my* faith, I needed to know more about *his*.

"Dude," I said, "someone's gotta tell these people they're being deceived."

"That's the thing, P," Gary explained. "They think we're the ones being deceived. That's why the Bible tells us we need to be prepared to defend what we believe."

"Where's it say that?" I asked, reaching for my Bible.

"First Peter 3:15, bro. Peter says that we must always be prepared to make a defense to anyone who asks for a reason for the hope that is in us. That's where the word *apologetics* comes from," he explained. "*Apologia* is Greek for 'make a defense.'"

That just about leveled me. I hadn't defended my faith at all. I didn't even know I was supposed to. I was starting to understand how Gary felt that day in the car—like I had let Jesus down.

We talked for a few more minutes, and then Gary gave me a list of websites where I could find out more about Jehovah's Witnesses, as well as some links to articles by popular Christian scholars and a bunch of Bible passages he wanted me to read. By the time we hung up, I was a furnace burning with zeal and passion. I couldn't hush my mind. I felt like there was so much I needed to learn. How, in the span of one afternoon, did I go from being Jesus' best spokesperson on campus to that dude in the back of the class who never has his homework done?

If I learned one thing from my first encounter with John, it's that I needed to be prepared to defend my faith, and part of that was knowing more about what he believed. How could I make John, a Jehovah's Witness, see the truth about Jesus if I didn't understand the false ways he was seeing him?

As I learned from Gary, this is the work of apologetics. Yet whenever the word *apologetics* gets used, I think Christians get intimidated, thinking they have to know Scripture backwards and forwards or have read the Bible from cover to cover ten times over or have studied all there is to know about a subject. But that's not really necessary. Apologetics is really about loving the Lord and being willing to tell other people about it. In fact, apologetics (defending the faith) has its roots in evangelism (sharing our faith). The two aren't synonymous, but they definitely hold hands. You can't really do one without the other. You tell someone you're a Christian, and you're an evangelist. But as soon as they ask a follow-up question, boom—you're an apologist. The answer you give—even if the conversation isn't as in-your-face as mine was with John—is a defense.

It's like when Gary and I would go out and hoop in the hood. He would simply make it known that he was a Christian, and some people would express their distrust for the church. People would be like "Christians are hypocrites" or "I can never trust those bogus pastors." They had seen too many "pastors" with Cadillacs and gold watches using slick words and collection plates to rob poor Black people for so long. That gave Gary not only an opening to talk about the gospel but also a responsibility to defend the church he called family. He would admit how some so-called pastors who love money more than people have snuck their stingy hearts into the church. But he would encourage them to look to Jesus and to not reject the church because of Judas. That he, too, was sick of seeing poor Black people being taken advantage of, but how the true church is indeed the bride of the God who created Black folk in his image. For a lot of people, Gary was the first person who made the church look good. These conversations were not argumentative, but his plea for them to see the true church was still a defense of the church and his faith.

> **YOU TELL SOMEONE YOU'RE A CHRISTIAN, AND YOU'RE AN EVANGELIST. BUT AS SOON AS THEY ASK A FOLLOW-UP QUESTION, BOOM—YOU'RE AN APOLOGIST.**

For years I led my church in what is sometimes called street evangelism. We would walk up to people we didn't know and start conversations about God. As it happens, my church was also in the hood where there were a lot of Jehovah's Witnesses, Mormons, and Hebrew Israelites seeking to reach us with their messages. So we had to spend a fair amount of time studying other religions and what they believe, because when Jesus tells us that we are to "make disciples of all nations," what he is really saying is that we need to make disciples of all *people*. Well, people from different backgrounds who subscribe to all kinds of religious doctrines are included in these people. We didn't avoid them because we were unfamiliar with their gods. We talked to them and studied what they believed. And the more we understood what they believed, the easier it was to know how to approach them with the truth.

Now, if you want an example of someone who did this well, look no further than the apostle Paul. He was brilliant. But more than that, he was faithful. He spoke several different languages, understood all kinds of philosophies, and was familiar with a bunch of different religious beliefs. And he used that knowledge to point out contradictions between the Christian faith and what the non-Christians of his day believed.

A classic example of this is in Acts 17. Paul was in Athens, where most of the population worshiped many different gods. After taking note of all the shrines and statues they'd built to honor their gods, he began to talk to people about Jesus, and he was brought before the ruling council of Athens. He told them, "Men of Athens, I perceive that in every way you are very religious. For as I passed along and observed the objects of your worship, I found also an altar with this inscription: 'To the unknown god'" (Acts 17:22-23).

Now normally when Paul preached, he opened with a quick review of Jewish history. But in this case, because he was in Athens, he knew his audience would neither understand nor appreciate it. So instead, he found a different entry point—one that had its roots in their own religion. You see, Paul knew that the Athenians built statues and shrines to curry favor with the gods, so when he discovered that they had built a shrine to an "unknown god" just to cover their bases, Paul wisely pounced on that as an opportunity to tell them about the one true God:

> What therefore you worship as unknown, this I
> proclaim to you. The God who made the world and
> everything in it, being Lord of heaven and earth, does
> not live in temples made by man, nor is he served by
> human hands, as though he needed anything, since
> he himself gives to all mankind life and breath and
> everything. And he made from one man every nation
> of mankind to live on all the face of the earth, having
> determined allotted periods and the boundaries of their
> dwelling place, that they should seek God, and perhaps
> feel their way toward him and find him. Yet he is
> actually not far from each one of us, for "In him we live
> and move and have our being"; as even some of your
> own poets have said, "For we are indeed his offspring."
> ACTS 17:23-28

You see what Paul did there? He used the poets his audience knew to speak their language to point them to his God. He then closed by playing on their fear of angering the gods and incurring their wrath:

> We ought not to think that the divine being is like
> gold or silver or stone, an image formed by the art
> and imagination of man. The times of ignorance
> God overlooked, but now he commands all people
> everywhere to repent, because he has fixed a day on
> which he will judge the world in righteousness by a
> man whom he has appointed; and of this he has given
> assurance to all by raising him from the dead.
>
> ACTS 17:29-31

I love how Paul carefully carried both truth and wisdom, not putting down one to operate in the other. And it brings to mind something he told the Corinthian believers: "I have become all things to all people, that by all means I might save some" (1 Corinthians 9:22). Paul was actively looking for opportunities to connect what he knew about his audience to the truth about Jesus.

Now I'm not saying you need to obsessively research every religion under the sun. In fact, I think that's where a lot of apologists go wrong. They try so hard to be jacks-of-all-trades that they end up being masters of none. I am, however, a firm believer in understanding the beliefs of the specific people you are trying to reach. In other words, if you don't live near a lot of Jehovah's Witnesses, Mormons, or Hebrew Israelites, don't knock yourself out studying what they believe. But if you feel like God is calling you to reach out to the Muslim family down the street, familiarize yourself with the Koran and the five pillars of Islam. You don't have to know everything, but if you don't know anything about what they believe, it's hard to know where their beliefs come into conflict with Christianity.

For example, a lot of the doctrines that Mormons and Jehovah's Witnesses believe have their origins in Christianity, so on the surface, it can sound like we believe the same thing—which is why I didn't understand at first that John was a Jehovah's Witness. He told me he was a Christian. If you don't know the distinctions between the two religions, you could easily think, *Oh, this person doesn't need to hear the gospel message.* Or worse, if you're not rock-solid in your own faith, they might be able to get you to question what you believe.

Because I know Jehovah's Witnesses take issue with the divinity of Jesus, when I share my faith with a Jehovah's Witness, I typically focus my energy on defending the Trinity. The same goes with the Mormons' take on salvation, Hebrew Israelites' emphasis on how keeping the law justifies us in God's eyes, and atheists' issues with God's will and the question of good and evil. When you know the distinctives between different religions and Christianity, it takes some of the pressure off because you don't have to know everything. You just need to know some key verses that address the main points of contention. The Holy Spirit will do the rest.

And I think that's another place where we can go wrong

when we share our faith with people: we don't trust the Holy Spirit's work. Instead, we develop a savior complex. We think that if our conversation doesn't end with the Sinner's Prayer, we've failed somehow. But it's the Spirit of God that gives life—not our intellect, our words, or our ability to debate or convince. I truly believe that God wants to raise up a generation of evangelists who are okay with being seed planters.

We need to take the pressure off ourselves and truly believe that the Spirit of God is indeed working—moving in the places we can't see. I might walk away from a conversation with a Jehovah's Witness with him still laughing that I believe Jesus is actually God, but what if while we were talking, God dropped a seed in the soil of his heart? I may have said something in our conversation that was a seed God wants to water tomorrow, or ten years from now. Remember, the first time I heard the gospel in a house church, I didn't give my life to the Lord. But God used a preacher in a living room to plant a seed of faith that Gary would one day water. In many ways, the church has conditioned us to expect right-now results. We send up praise shouts for how many bodies ran to the altar when the pastor said to come. For some of us, hearing testimonies about how people came to faith can be the highlight of our day. But what if God wants to raise up a generation of evangelists who are content with not seeing the fruit of their labor until they get to glory?

Believe it or not, this call is for all believers. I'm not saying that everyone needs to be a street evangelist. While we are all called to obey the great commission, we're not all called to

WE THINK THAT IF OUR CONVERSATION DOESN'T END WITH THE SINNER'S PRAYER, WE'VE FAILED SOMEHOW. BUT IT'S THE SPIRIT OF GOD THAT GIVES LIFE—NOT OUR INTELLECT, OUR WORDS, OR OUR ABILITY TO DEBATE OR CONVINCE.

fulfill it in that way. When Peter tells believers that they should "always [be] prepared to make a defense to anyone who asks you for a reason for the hope that is in you" (1 Peter 3:15), he isn't telling us to start arguing with people. (In fact, we'll look at the last words of that verse in chapter 4.) He's simply telling us that we need to be prepared when the opportunity to defend our faith arises.

Because make no mistake: no matter where you live, at some point, you will be called upon to share or defend your faith with somebody who's operating from a different belief system than you, whether it's the fallen-away Catholic who lives next door, the yoga instructor at your health club who says she's really starting to get into Buddhism, or your agnostic uncle who's always making his opinions known at family get-togethers. The goal of "always being prepared" isn't to become some kind of Bible Jedi Master, ready to take on any and all objections at once. The goal is to tell the truth of the gospel to others to win hearts, not arguments. It's to tell the truth in a way that represents God well without it turning into a shouting match, without you completely turning people off, and without you sounding like you don't know what you're talking about. We'll talk more about some of the particulars of how to do that in later chapters.

The people who are doing it right are the ones who really understand the great commission. They can look at people who are part of a religious cult, who claim God doesn't exist, or who are out there shouting false prophecies from a street corner, and rather than getting defensive or upset, they say, "God loves these people and wants to reach them." And from the very beginning, the way he reaches them is through us, his followers.

I know that feels like a lot of pressure. And I know a lot of believers avoid talking with non-Christians about their faith because they're afraid they'll mess it up. But if there's one thing I've learned from countless encounters with people of different faiths, it's that our God is great enough to use even our worst mistakes for his glory. This doesn't mean we don't need to try to understand the people we're talking to or what they believe. But it does mean that God uses even imperfect Christians to make himself known in the world.

I've talked about my community and what trying to reach them involves. But what about the people who live near you? Who are they, and what do they believe? What will it look like for you to be "prepared to make a defense . . . for the hope that is in you" to the people that God has placed in your way? You don't have to know everything, but what might be helpful for you to learn to answer the questions they might have about your faith?

3

THE ESSENTIALS YOU NEED TO KNOW

As soon as Gary and I finished our call discussing what happened with John, I went straight to the Internet to check out the sites he had given me. I was a man motivated by my wounded pride and bruised ego. To be frank, Johnny boy had me messed up. Not only did he embarrass me, but I also felt like I had lost a battle for God and had to redeem myself to make God proud.

I learned through my research that the Jehovah's Witnesses traced their roots back to a guy named Charles Taze Russell, a millionaire who owned a bunch of clothing stores in Pennsylvania in the late 1800s. Though he grew up a devout Presbyterian, Russell began to question his faith in his teens because he couldn't reconcile the idea of a merciful God condemning people to hell. He eventually latched on to a group of Adventist preachers prophesying that the world would end in 1878, sold his clothing stores, and used the money to publish religious journals warning people about Christ's impending return.

When the world didn't end in 1878, Russell founded the Watch Tower Bible and Tract Society to publish and disseminate, among other things, his own revised prediction that the world would end in 1914. And even though his prediction didn't come true, because he was such a charismatic figure, he amassed a large and loyal following and encouraged them to go door-to-door, preaching to their neighbors that the day of reckoning was coming.

After Russell died in 1916, several factions developed within the larger group, one of which became the Jehovah's Witnesses, who still use the Watch Tower Bible and Tract Society to publish their materials today.

None of this sat well with me, especially the idea of making false predictions about the end of the world. I looked up what the Bible had to say about prophecies that didn't come true and found Deuteronomy 18:22: "When a prophet speaks in the name of the LORD, if the word does not come to pass or come true, that is a word that the LORD has not spoken."

Man, I thought, *that whole religion is based on the teachings of a false prophet!*

After cross-checking what I'd found against several other sites, I scribbled a few notes down and thought I was war ready. You couldn't convince me that, with the little research I had in my arsenal, I wasn't prepared for battle. I sat at the computer and imagined my mouth being a pistol the next day, my jaw cocked and ready and my tongue loaded with truth to aim at John. My eyes were two swords ready to cut him deep with every stare. To top it off, because I thought I was doing the Lord's work, I just knew God would be my shield. With the Lord on my pride—I mean, my side—I was ready to take John down.

Or so I thought.

The next day at school, I found John in the cafeteria and went in hard. "Man, I think you're in a cult, bro."

His sarcastic laugh returned to haunt me. "What makes you think that?"

"I did some research last night about Charles Taze Russell, and that dude was off, bro! Dude was a false prophet!" I said it loud enough to make sure everyone in the vicinity could hear.

John smirked, pitying me with his gaze. "Charles Taze Russell is *not* our leader. *Jehovah* is our leader."

I shot back, "Nah, bruh. Everything you believe started with his teachings!"

"Preston," he said with all the calm his voice could muster, "Charles Taze Russell did not start the Jehovah's Witnesses. He died two years before the Jehovah's Witnesses were founded. He's not our leader. We believe Jesus is our Savior, just like you do."

This was not going at all how I'd planned. I looked down at my notes, almost all of which focused on Charles Taze Russell's false prophecies.

"We get baptized in Jesus' name," John continued, "we love Jesus, and we believe that Jesus is the person that God sent—just like you do."

Nah, I thought. *This dude is trying to play me. That can't be right.* It was harder now to stay afloat. It felt like I was drowning. I quickly glanced at my notes again and saw a small glimmer of hope, like a lighthouse in the distance. "But Russell said that only 144,000 followers would make it into heaven. We believe Jesus died for *all* our sins."

"First off," John said curtly, "we also believe Jesus died for all sins! Charles Russell didn't say that only 144,000 followers would make it into heaven. Revelation 7:4 says that 144,000 of all the tribes of the children of Israel will enter into heaven. And second—"

"Preston, is this boy talking crazy to you again?" I looked up to find Brittany had locked eyes with John, our friends Dion and Junior behind her, looking to see a good fight.

John smirked. "I'm not talking crazy to anyone. Preston and I are just talking about Jesus."

"Oh, okay. Well, Preston knows way more about Jesus than you do!" Brittany was a loyal friend, but she didn't know her way around the Bible that well. And truthfully, neither did I.

"Really?" John's smirk cut deeper, then he nodded at the paper in my hand. "Is that why he came back with notes?"

Heat began to rise like an anger revolution on the back of my neck.

"Listen, Preston," he continued, "yesterday you said that Jesus is God almighty, right?"

"Yeah."

He pointed at my notes again. "You got proof of that?"

"Yeah, I do." I opened my Bible to Philippians 2:10-11 again. "See, right here it says, 'Every knee should bow, in heaven and on earth and under the earth, and every tongue confess that Jesus Christ is Lord.'"

"Then how do you explain this?" he said, pointing to the verse right above it. "It says, 'Christ Jesus, who, though he was in the form of God, did not count equality with God a thing to be grasped, but emptied himself, by taking the form of a servant, being born in the likeness of men. And being found in human form, he humbled himself by becoming obedient to the point of death, even death on a cross.' How can Jesus be *obedient* to God and *be* God at the same time?"

"That's . . ." *That's a good question*, I wanted to respond, but my whole body became a stutter. My heart began beating to the sound of defeat. I looked around at the faces rooting for me to win and felt bad that I was letting them down again. "You're misinterpreting that" was the only comeback I could think of.

He sat back. "Well, how *should* I interpret it then?"

I said nothing. I folded my notes along with my dignity and put them back in my book bag. They didn't matter anymore. Pretty much everything I'd written down was intended to prove that the Jehovah's Witnesses were a cult founded by a false prophet. I felt so defeated.

"You went home and studied," John said. "That's fine. But you didn't answer my questions."

I was so angry. The dude beat up my ego—again.

Looking back, I can tell you exactly where I messed up that day. After my first conversation with John, what I should have done was go home and pray. I should have sought the Father with a fist full of humility and asked him to help lead me in showing John the truth. God's divine wisdom will always lead us to where we need to go if we would just pause and ask him the way. Second, I should have studied the Scriptures. God and the Word written with his Spirit had all the right answers for John. Instead, I spent the whole night researching the Jehovah's Witnesses and looking for dirt on Charles Taze Russell. Almost all my notes revolved around proving the Jehovah's Witnesses were a cult, because in my mind, the only way to prove that what I believed was right was to show John that what he believed was wrong. In other words, I didn't walk into that cafeteria ready to defend my faith; I walked in ready to attack his.

I DIDN'T WALK INTO THAT CAFETERIA READY TO DEFEND MY FAITH; I WALKED IN READY TO ATTACK HIS.

Instead of taking my time and really interrogating the

Scriptures to build up my own faith, I wanted to interrogate John to tear down his. Instead of studying what others had to say, sitting with it, processing it, and finding the right words to explain why I believed what I believed, I rushed right back into battle foolishly naked, thinking I had the right armor for war. I was overconfident and underprepared, and—if I'm being honest—more concerned with defending my reputation than defending my faith.

The problem is, just proving someone else is wrong doesn't automatically prove you're right. You still have to be able to articulate why your beliefs make sense, and I still had no idea how to do that.

As we looked at in the last chapter, there is value in studying other religions, or at the very least, familiarizing yourself with what other people believe. I just went about it the wrong way. Before I met John, I had been the evangelist at my school who really wanted to reach people with the gospel. But I wasn't seeking the wisdom I needed that could help me reach John. I was looking for weapons to harm him the way he had harmed my ego.

Now that we've seen the value of understanding what other people believe, I hope to help you understand and articulate some of our own Christian beliefs. As I've mentioned throughout this book, you don't have to be studied up in every part of Christian faith and doctrine to be able to talk to others about Jesus, but you should have a clear handle on the foundational beliefs of who Jesus is and salvation by faith alone in Christ alone. Let's look at those aspects of our faith.

The central question for many people is "Who is Jesus?" And honestly, that's the perfect place to start, because if you can't explain who Jesus is and why he is Lord, everything else falls apart.

The reason Jesus is the lynchpin in any discussion about faith is because he brings everybody to a decision. You can say you believe in God all day long, and atheists aside, most religions won't question it. But once you say, "I believe *Jesus* is God," bruh, it's on.

Paul Washer says, "We hypocritically applaud men for seeking the truth, but call for the public execution of anyone arrogant enough to believe he has found it."[1] I've found this to be especially true once you say that Jesus is God. Jesus was attacked when he claimed to be God (see John 10:31). And the world will attack us as well for the very same reason.

The problem isn't that other religions don't believe Jesus existed. It's that they don't believe he is God.

- Hebrew Israelites believe he was a man—which he was. (See John 1:14.)
- Muslims believe he was a prophet—which he was. (See John 7:40; Acts 3:22; Hebrews 1:1-2.)
- Mormons believe he was God's Son—which he was. (See Matthew 3:17.)
- Jehovah's Witnesses believe he's the way, the truth, and the life—which he is. (See John 14:6.)

JUST PROVING
SOMEONE ELSE IS
WRONG DOESN'T
AUTOMATICALLY
PROVE YOU'RE
RIGHT. YOU STILL
HAVE TO BE ABLE
TO ARTICULATE
WHY YOUR BELIEFS
MAKE SENSE.

None of them deny his existence. They just deny his deity. Jesus was fully human. He was a prophet. He was a son. And he is our Savior. He's all of these things. But he's also God in the flesh, and understanding that changes everything. If Jesus is God, it means that Jesus didn't just offer some good teachings that we can decide to follow if we choose. It means that he is the Lord, our authority, and we owe him our worship and allegiance.

Let's start the conversation about Jesus' deity by looking at how I might have answered John's question from Philippians 2 about how Jesus could both be God and be obedient to God at the same time. Granted, I didn't know this at the time, but what might I have said if I had gone home to study Scripture?

John was essentially arguing that if Jesus was really God, he couldn't give up equality with God, and if he was really God, there's no way he would have to become obedient to someone else.

But it helps to look at the context of the passage. Right before the passage John and I were arguing about, Paul tells the Philippian church, "Do nothing from selfish ambition or conceit, but in humility count others more significant than yourselves. . . . Have this mind among yourselves, which is yours in Christ Jesus" (Philippians 2:3, 5).

Paul's main point in getting the Philippians to think about Jesus "empt[ying] himself, by taking the form of a servant" (Philippians 2:7) is to point them to Jesus' great humility so that they can imitate it. So the question is, why is Jesus "not count[ing] equality with God a thing to be grasped" (verse 6) an example of great humility?

Well, let me first explain why I believe John and so many other Jehovah's Witnesses misunderstand what the apostle Paul wrote here. They believe Jesus is displaying humility by merely knowing his place, as if Jesus were saying, "Father, you are God and I am not. I humbly submit to you to the point of death." The problem with that logic is that's not at all what humility is. Humility is not someone merely knowing their place. It is someone recognizing that they have certain rights and privileges but being willing to give them up to serve someone else. For example, famous singers have certain privileges that non-famous singers do not have—access to better gigs and bigger venues, as well as connections to other big names in the business. How can a famous singer serve singers who aren't famous? One way is to give up some of their privileges to serve these other singers. This can look like a famous singer giving up a spot to perform at the Oscars to a singer with less recognition or sharing the stage with another singer on tour. Jesus is displaying great humility because he's giving up the privileges and rights he has always had as God in order to serve others (*us*).

It says next that Jesus "emptied himself, by taking the form of a servant" (verse 7). Through the years I've talked to many Jehovah's Witnesses and other religious groups who think that those who believe Jesus is God must believe that Jesus stopped being God when he emptied himself and became a human servant. They ask questions like "So when Jesus emptied himself, do you believe he emptied himself of his divine nature? Can God stop being God?" I've even had Jehovah's Witnesses tell me that can be the only logical explanation to my beliefs.

But that's not what orthodox Christians believe. God will not and cannot stop being God. Jesus didn't empty himself of divinity, but he emptied himself of the rights he had always had as God. I love how the King James Version says he "made himself of no reputation," meaning he set the privileges of who he was aside. He didn't give up who he was and has always been. If you believe Jesus is not God, it is easy to assume that Christians believe Jesus had to empty himself of his divine nature to become human. But let's revisit the famous singer who gives up their privileges to serve non-famous singers. When that happens, the famous singer doesn't stop being famous. Their nature doesn't change just because they voluntarily gave up some of their privileges. In the same way, just because Jesus gave up his privileges as God doesn't mean his nature changed.

The text says that Jesus was "in the form of God" but "did not count equality with God a thing to be grasped" (verse 6). In other words, Jesus didn't consider his status as equal with God as something to cling tightly to. If Jesus had equality with God in his grasp, we can imagine the great humility it took to let it go. The point is, Jesus *did* have equality with God the Father but let a lot of his privileges go in order to serve those he created.

Let me put it to you like this. If you, I, or any other created being "did not count equality with God a thing to be grasped," it wouldn't be humility; it would be reality, because we never had equality with God to begin with. Jesus being willing to let this equality go was such great humility because he has had equality with the Father for all of eternity. "How?" you might ask. Because Jesus is God (see John 17:5).

The next question we should ask ourselves is "How did Jesus let these privileges go?" Philippians goes on to say that Jesus let go of these privileges by "being found in human form." Jesus was fully God on earth but was also fully human (see Colossians 2:9). In his humanity Jesus had to naturally let go of a lot of his privileges as God. Jesus, for the first time in all of eternity, experientially knew what it felt like to be physically tired. For the first time he needed food made by the same human hands he whispered from the dust. Jesus had to depend on a woman he created to nurse him so he could become the man who would die for us all.

The crucial truth to grasp here is that God didn't send somebody else; God sent his Son, the second member of the triune God, to die for us. God himself came to die for sinners like you and me. No other God can say that. No other religion can say their God stepped off his throne to save the people he created except Christianity.

GOD DIDN'T SEND SOMEBODY ELSE; GOD SENT HIS SON, THE SECOND MEMBER OF THE TRIUNE GOD, TO DIE FOR US.

The next thing we see in this text is Jesus became obedient to death. The Jehovah's Witnesses don't believe Jesus is God but instead believe he is the first and greatest being created by Jehovah. Hear me when I say this, though: ordinary humans do not *become* "obedient to death." They are *already* subject to death. If you are human, you can and will die one day. Jesus had to become "obedient to death" because for all eternity, he was superior over death. In fact, Jesus never knew death and death never knew him before he wrapped himself in flesh.

Jesus is and always has been an eternal being. This great love and humility is why the end of the text tells us the Father has given Jesus "the name that is above every name, so that at the name of Jesus every knee should bow, in heaven and on earth and under the earth, and every tongue confess that Jesus Christ is Lord, to the glory of God the Father" (Philippians 2:9-11).

So we see Jesus' divinity in Philippians 2, but it's also all over the New Testament. One of the best descriptions of Jesus' divinity also comes from the apostle Paul. He writes,

> [Jesus] is the image of the invisible God, the firstborn of all creation. For by him all things were created, in heaven and on earth, visible and invisible, whether thrones or dominions or rulers or authorities—all things were created through him and for him. And he is before all things, and in him all things hold together. And he is the head of the body, the church. He is the beginning, the firstborn from the dead, that in everything he might be preeminent. For in him all the fullness of God was pleased to dwell, and through him to reconcile to himself all things, whether on earth or in heaven, making peace by the blood of his cross.
>
> COLOSSIANS 1:15-20

I love this passage because it covers just about everything other religions take issue with when it comes to Jesus. Let's look at a few key parts.

First, Paul says that Jesus "is the image of the invisible God."

If you look at the opening passage of the Gospel of John, you'll see that John echoes the opening of Genesis 1 and refers to Jesus as both "the Word" and "God": "In the beginning was the Word, and the Word was with God, and the Word was God" (John 1:1).

This isn't a coincidence. John does this specifically to make the point that Jesus and God are one and that they have been since time began. He then goes on to say, "The Word became flesh and dwelt among us, and we have seen his glory, glory as of the only Son from the Father, full of grace and truth" (John 1:14).

In other words, Jesus is God in the flesh, just as Paul describes him.

Next, Paul says that Jesus is "the firstborn of all creation." Now, that doesn't mean that Jesus was simply physically born, the way we are, or that he is God's creation. Jehovah's Witnesses can sometimes get hung up on that. They would argue that since Jesus is "the firstborn of all creation," he is, by definition, created by God and therefore cannot be God.

But if we look at the way that term is used elsewhere in the Bible (for example, in Psalm 89:27), we see that it really refers to authority—being supreme or in charge. So when Paul refers to Jesus as "the firstborn of all creation," he is actually stating that Jesus is *Lord* over all creation. As Jesus says after his resurrection, "All authority in heaven and on earth has been given to me" (Matthew 28:18). And Jesus is consistently referred to as "Lord" throughout the New Testament (see, for example, Acts 2:36; Romans 10:9; 1 Peter 3:15; Revelation 17:14).

Paul goes on to say of Jesus, "He is before all things, and in him all things hold together. . . . He is the beginning, . . . that in everything he might be preeminent. For in him all the fullness of God was pleased to dwell" (Colossians 1:17-19). I want to camp out here for a little bit because Paul is hitting at something with these statements that a lot of religions take issue with, and that's the Trinity.

When Paul wrote this, he was challenging those who did not believe Jesus could be fully human and fully divine at the same time—in other words, that he could not be both Jesus the man and Jesus the member of the Godhead.

Now, we've already talked about how Jesus and God were both present "in the beginning" and how Jesus is "God in the flesh." To take that a step further, when we say that Jesus is God, we are not saying that Jesus and God are the same person. What we are saying is that Jesus and God (and the Holy Spirit) share the same essence, and in that sense, they are one. They all are equally God, coexisting as three distinct but equal persons. Sharing the same essence is not the same as being the same person. The Father is not the Son. The Son is not the Father. And the Father is not the Holy Spirit.

That's a lot to take in, right? Well, the good news is that the air God created is free, so just breathe. We're gonna get through this together. But that's why this concept features in so many apologetic arguments. It's easy to get all twisted up. Ask any Jehovah's Witness or Mormon who Jesus is, and they'll tell you he's the Son of God. And in a way, they're right. Jesus *is* God's Son. But not in the way we think of it—not in the way that

Maverick Perry is my dad, I am his son, and he existed before I was born.

The thing is, God doesn't exist like you and me. He just doesn't. That's why our "human" analogies don't work. For example, some people try to explain the Trinity by saying that God plays three different roles in the same way that water can exist as a liquid, a solid, or a vapor. Seems logical enough, but what they're describing isn't accurate. In fact, it's heretical. God isn't one dude who plays three different parts. He didn't start off as God, then change into Jesus for a while, then go back to being God again. God didn't stop being one thing to become something else in the same way that water stops being a liquid to become steam or ice. God has always been God, he has always been Jesus, and he has always been the Holy Spirit. To try to explain it any other way is heretical because it strips Jesus of his divinity.

The Bible is clear that God is a Trinity—three distinct persons sharing one nature.

The Trinity can seem like an academic topic, but truly, this is foundational for our belief in God, first, because it reveals that Jesus is God. It's also foundational because we believe, as John tells us, that "God is love" (1 John 4:16). But love requires someone to love. God doesn't change, and he has been love from the beginning, even before Creation. God, in the community of the three persons of the Trinity—Father, Son, and Holy Spirit—has always been (and will always be) love.

Let me put it this way: if love is an attribute that can only be expressed by loving another person, God cannot be a God of love if he existed alone with no one to actively love. So when other religions deny the triune God of Scripture, they are not only claiming that Jesus and the Holy Spirit aren't equally God with the Father. They are also saying that they serve a God who at one time was loveless, a God who at one time existed alone with no one to love.

Another key aspect of our faith is that we are saved by faith in Jesus, not by the good works we might do. We believe that we could never do enough to earn God's salvation; it has to be given to us as a free gift through the work of Jesus Christ. And as you would expect for something so foundational to our belief, this often comes in conflict with other religions.

I believe the religions that attempt to work for their own salvation do so because they fundamentally misunderstand the first point, that Jesus is God. If we don't understand that our sin is so offensive to a holy and righteous God that it took God himself to come and die for his own creation, it can be hard to fully understand the grace of God. And if we don't understand the grace of God, we will think that our salvation has to include our works on top of the finished work of Jesus. If you get Jesus wrong, everything starts to fall apart. But if we get Jesus right, everything will start to make sense.

One day, while I was walking around in a nearby neighborhood, I ran into two young Latter-day Saints who were out doing their required two-year missionary journey. They wore crispy white-collar shirts, void of spots and wrinkles, just like the church Christ will come back for, contrasted with jet-black dress pants ironed to perfection. Their haircuts were neatly fresh like they'd just walked out of the barbershop. I could tell they believed their presentation before they spoke.

After taking the time to get to know them a little, we started talking about Jesus, and before I knew it, we were camped out at a picnic table in a nearby park, chopping it up about the distinctions between Mormonism and Christianity. I have to be honest, I was not as informed about Mormonism as I was with other religions I have engaged with in the neighborhoods I've lived in. Because of that, I spent a while asking them questions to understand what they believe. But there were some things I did know about the LDS faith, one of those being what the Book of Mormon said about works as it pertains to our salvation. They kept insisting that we basically believed that we are saved by grace, so I asked them about that.

I showed them one of the verses I had run across from the Book of Mormon, 2 Nephi 25:23: "We labor diligently to write, to persuade our children, and also our brethren, to believe in Christ, and to be reconciled to God; for we know that it is by grace that we are saved, after all we can do."

They looked at me like *What's the big deal? It says we are saved by grace.* But I felt led by God to challenge them. "See?" I said. "That's where we disagree."

"How so?" one of them asked.

I opened my Bible to Ephesians 2:8-9. "The Bible says, 'For by grace you have been saved through faith. And this is not your own doing; it is the gift of God, not a result of works, so that no one may boast.'"

"Exactly." He smiled proudly, as if he were teaching something about God while God was watching. "We both believe we are saved by grace."

"You're right that we both believe we are saved by grace," I conceded, "but your book also says, '*after* all we can do.' Doesn't that imply that we have to work for it?"

They looked at each other for a second, then the older one replied, "Well, we believe that God gives us grace to do the work, but he wants us to work. He wants us to be diligent. He wants us to be faithful, and he wants us to honor him with our work."

"Well," I said, "with all due respect, the Bible teaches us that there isn't any type or amount of work we can do that would be good enough to earn our salvation. Grace doesn't just fill in the gaps in our work. Salvation is God's work, start to finish. That's why God had to send someone perfect to do the work on our behalf. That's why it's called a gift from God."

He thought about that for a second, then opened his Bible. "What about that verse in James?" he asked, flipping through the pages. "The one that says, 'Faith without works is dead.' What do you think that means?"

I knew exactly which verse he was referring to. "You mean James 2:17?"

"Yes!" His mouth opened wide with excitement as he found the Scripture to show me. These boys were young, with zeal spilling from their ears. They were so eager to teach me what they believed was the truth. I knew I had to handle their young hearts with care while showing them how I believe what they've been taught is wrong. "So also faith by itself," he began, "if it does not have works, is dead." He looked up at me. "Seems pretty self-explanatory, doesn't it?"

"No," I said. "Can you explain it to me?"

"Well," he started, "it means that if we don't do good work . . ."—he paused, then looked to the sky to find the right words—"our work basically dies. So, it's like we're wasting our life."

"See, I don't think that's what that verse means," I said. "Our works are not what justify us in the eyes of God; they're evidence that we have been justified. They aren't justification for the grace we've been given; they're an outpouring of the grace we've received. God doesn't look at our works and say, 'Because you did the good work, you're justified.' He says, 'Because you believed in my Son, you are justified.' It doesn't mean that if we don't work, our faith dies. It means that if we don't have evidence of good works, we probably never had faith to begin with. That means that we are still dead spiritually."

My Mormon friends aren't alone in struggling with this concept. Virtually every religion in the world teaches that we have to work to please God and earn our salvation. Jews believe they must adhere to a lengthy list of laws

EVERY RELIGION IN THE WORLD HAS FOUND SOMETHING TO WORK FOR TO PLEASE GOD. CHRISTIANITY IS THE ONLY FAITH THAT SAYS THE GOD WHO FINISHED THE WORK HAS FOUND ME.

and customs to please God. Muslims believe they must pray five times a day, fast, give alms, pledge allegiance to Muhammad, and make a pilgrimage to Mecca. Hindus believe they must purify themselves. And Buddhists believe they must renounce all worldly things and die to self in order to achieve nirvana.

Christianity is the only religion where the work of salvation has already been done for us. Every religion in the world has found something to work for to please God. Christianity is the only faith that says the God who finished the work has found me.

All we have to do is "confess with [our] mouth that Jesus is Lord and believe in [our] heart that God raised him from the dead," and Romans 10:9 assures us that "[we] will be saved."

In fact, God makes it clear what he thinks of our attempts to win his approval through works when he speaks through the prophet Isaiah: "We have all become like one who is unclean, and all our righteous deeds are like a polluted garment" (Isaiah 64:6). It turns out that our good works are no good to God. Now, don't hear me say that God doesn't want Christians to display good works. He indeed does. God just doesn't accept our works as it pertains to our salvation. He only accepts the finished work of Jesus alone.

How we are saved isn't the only point of disagreement between Christianity and other religions. They also disagree about *who* can be saved.

If you live in an urban area, or anywhere Black faces are often seen, you can find Hebrew Israelites trying to awaken what they call the "sleeping children of Israel." Hebrew Israelites are one of the fastest-growing religions in America right now, in large part because they have a massive appeal among Black millennials and Gen Zers. I've spent years trying to reach them. If my relationship with John taught me anything, it's that understanding the people I'm trying to reach is equally important as understanding what they believe. Coming from a place where mostly Black bodies dwell, I found this truth to be most relevant when engaging with Hebrew Israelites. In the Black community, our evangelism and the way we engage in apologetics looks different than engaging with other faith groups. When I was debating John every week in college, all of our conversations centered mostly around theology. But in my talks with Hebrew Israelites, I quickly found out how much systemic and social issues helped create and fueled the flame of Hebrew Israelism.

Hebrew Israelites teach that they are the direct descendants of the lost children of Israel, that they were sold into slavery by Africans, and that all of the injustices that have befallen Black people over the centuries are a direct result of their ancestors not keeping the Ten Commandments (see Deuteronomy 4:27; 28:15-68). They believe they have a chance to keep God's law, and in doing so God will keep them. You can sometimes find them downtown in big cities looking for Black people to witness to. But Black neighborhoods are their main mission field.

They adhere very strictly to the King James Version and lean heavily on the teachings of the Old Testament. They also maintain that popular depictions of a white Jesus are deliberate attempts to steal their identity and that Christianity is a false religion.

Not all Hebrew Israelites are angry and loud, but a lot of camps are. They're angry about slavery. They're angry that Black people didn't always have the right to vote. They're angry that Blacks have historically been perceived as an inferior race. But hear me out: just because their theology is false doesn't mean their anger should be a reason to ignore the way they feel. In the same way I had to get to know John in order to empathize with him back in college, we, too, have to understand the pain some brown people feel that led them to reject the Christian faith and embrace Hebrew Israelism. In order to reach them, the last thing we should do is write them off as angry Black men and women. We should see each of them as stories. Black Christian leaders shouldn't sweep their pain under the pulpit but acknowledge it in hopes their empathy might lead some to the cross.

Needless to say, some Hebrew Israelite camps in America will tell you that white people cannot inherit the Kingdom of God. If you ask them why (which I have), they will likely respond with something along the lines of "Have you ever seen white people do good? Look what they did to the Native Americans. Look what they did to the children of Israel. Look what they're doing now!" In fact, they believe that when the Messiah does come, he will destroy white people, who they call "Edomites," or enemies of the descendants of Jacob (see Ezekiel 25:12-14).

But, like John and Paul, Mark 16:15-16 tells us that salvation is for all people. We are to "go into all the world and proclaim the gospel to the whole creation. Whoever believes and is baptized will be saved, but whoever does not believe will be condemned." God wants everyone—the whole of creation—to hear the Good News and be saved. He isn't checking the color of people's skin. Through the work of Jesus, he's throwing the doors wide open and saying to everyone, "Come on in!"

I don't know about you, but that's what I call Good News.

Again, I want to be clear: when you share your faith, you don't have to know everything, but it helps to keep your mind fixed on who Jesus is and how we are saved, because these are places where Christianity differs from all other religions. While religion is often seen as people searching for God, Christianity is the story of God searching for us because he loves us and wants to be in relationship with us.

With a story that has love at its center, you'd think that the desire to tell others about Jesus would always be an act of love. But as I was about to learn, my debates with John were anything but.

4

WINNING HEARTS, NOT ARGUMENTS

JOHN AND I KEPT MEETING in the cafeteria every Wednesday and Thursday, and for a long time, that dude picked apart my arguments with ease. It's like he knew the whole Bible and mastered the art of dismantling Christians' faith. Lucky for me, I was convinced that the God who met me that day in my room had unparched my thirsty soul forever. John couldn't take away my certainty that before God whispered the world into existence, he said, "Preston will be my son." Because of grace, my faith in Jesus was immovable as a stubborn mountain.

The Bible says that "faith is the assurance of things hoped for, the conviction of things not seen" (Hebrews 11:1). I had that faith part down. It was evidence that I lacked. Having faith without the proper evidence made me look like I was the one who was still blind in every debate I had with John. I was beginning to see that God didn't want me to have blind faith when he had provided his people with so much evidence. As time grew on us both, I didn't care how much information John knew. I knew that I'd had an encounter with the God of the universe. John's beliefs were sincere, but I believed he was sincerely wrong, and I was determined to prove that to him. Every night, I would go home and study, and within a few weeks, not only was I able to answer his questions, but I was also able to hit him with a few of my own.

Battling John at school became my drug. Every week I looked forward to our debates to get my fix. I became addicted to shutting John down. When I did, my high lasted for days. Every time we met, I would ask him questions, and when he couldn't answer them . . . I'm not gonna lie—I felt vindicated, like I was beating up the school bully who embarrassed me in the past.

John was obsessed with proving that Jesus and the Father are not equal. Well, one night I was reading in Revelation, and I noticed Jesus referred to himself as "the Alpha and the Omega, the first and the last, the beginning and the end" (Revelation 22:13), so the next time I saw John, I asked him point-blank how he would explain Jesus calling himself that.

"You in Revelation?" he asked.

"Yup," I said, with one of those *I'm about to get you back* smiles. *Let's talk about it, bro!*

"Look at 22:12," he said, with caution disguised as confidence. "It says, 'Behold, I am coming soon . . .'"

"Yeah?" *What's your point, bro?*

He tapped the page with his finger and said, "That's Jehovah talking, not Jesus."

I anticipated him saying that, so his words weren't fresh off his lips before I said, "Nope! Look what it says three verses down: 'I, Jesus, have sent my angel to testify to you about these things for the churches. I am the root and the descendant of David, the bright morning star' (Revelation 22:16)."

"I, Jesus," I repeated, tapping the verse like he did. John stared at the verse like a riddle. As he gathered his thoughts, I took advantage of his silence to hit with another point. "Jehovah's Witnesses believe that Jesus is the one the Father will send one day to judge the world, correct?"

"Yeah, because that's true," he replied.

"So we know this is Jesus talking because he starts the verse off saying, 'I am coming soon.'"

He waved me off. "Awww . . . you all point to that verse."

"That's because it's true!" I said, laughing. *Admit it, bro, you got nothing to say!*

"No, it ain't." He smiled and shook his head.

The dude was exasperating. "Fine," I said. "If Jesus isn't the Alpha and the Omega, then who is he?"

"Jesus is another name for Michael," he said calmly.

"Michael—the archangel?" I asked.

"Yeah," he said. "That's who Jehovah was talking to in Genesis. That's the 'we.'"

I cut him with my stare to let him know he had to work harder. "Dude, where are you getting that from?"

"First Thessalonians," he said, flipping back a few pages. "'The Lord himself will descend from heaven with a commanding call, with an archangel's voice' (1 Thessalonians 4:16)."[2]

"That doesn't say Jesus *is* the archangel," I said incredulously. "It just says he had the *voice* of one."

"But there's only one," he said. "Michael is always referred to as *the* archangel. Also, *arch* means 'chief,' meaning Michael was the head angel. Furthermore"—he leaned in and started riffling through his Bible; he was going for the kill—"Revelation 12:7 says, 'And war broke out in heaven and Michael and his angels battled with the dragon.' So, Michael is the leader of an army of angels. And Revelation 19:13 describes a man on a white horse called 'The Word of God,' who you say is Jesus. But the verse says that 'the armies of heaven followed him' (Revelation 19:14). So we've got two leaders of angels—one of whom is Michael and the other, 'Jesus,'" he said, using air quotes. "But the Bible doesn't say anything about there being two armies of angels—just one. So that means that Michael and Jesus are one and the same. They just have different names, like Simon/Peter or Saul/Paul. It's all right there, man." He closed his Bible halfway and smiled like he'd just nailed his sermon and I had to preach behind him.

Everyone was staring at me, waiting for me to respond. I glanced over at Dion and Junior. They both had that look that said, *Bruh, I know you ain't gonna let him talk to you like that!* To my left, Brittany looked like a supportive wife who just watched her husband go down in the ring, embarrassed for me but the hope in her eyes saying, *Get up, Preston! Get up and fight back!* And these were my most faithful supporters. Man, I'm telling you, it was tense. It was daunting.

It was . . . *exactly* the moment I'd been waiting for.

"Funny you should bring that up." I smiled, like the star in a Marvel movie getting up after everyone thought he was dead. I reached for my Bible and turned to the page I had bookmarked the night before. *Trying to put me on blast in front of everybody,* I scoffed to myself. *I knew you'd go for that archangel thing.*

What John didn't know was that as soon as I'd stumbled upon that Alpha and Omega verse in Revelation, I googled "How do Jehovah's Witnesses explain Revelation 22:13?" and it led me straight to the "Jesus is Michael" argument. So I did a little extra research. And I knew that if I let John play the argument out, let him think he'd beaten me again, he'd eventually end up right . . . "Here," I said, pointing to Hebrews 1:5-10. I even stood up for effect. "It says:

'For to which of the angels did God ever say,

"You are my Son,
    today I have begotten you"?

'Or again,

"I will be to him a father,
    and he shall be to me a son"?

'And again, when he brings the firstborn into the world, he says,

"Let all God's angels worship him."

'Of the angels he says,

"He makes his angels winds,
    and his ministers a flame of fire."

'But of the Son he says,

"Your throne, O God, is forever and ever,
    the scepter of uprightness is the scepter of your
        kingdom.
You have loved righteousness and hated wickedness;
therefore God, your God, has anointed you
    with the oil of gladness beyond your companions."

'And,

"You, Lord, laid the foundation of the earth in the
        beginning,
    and the heavens are the work of your hands.""'

John just stared at me like *Yeah . . . so?* I carefully laid it out for him. "First, it says that the Father has never called an angel a son. Second, it says that the Father told all angels to worship

Jesus. Third, the Father says that Jesus' throne will last forever and ever. And lastly, the Father says that Jesus created the earth as the work of his hands."

"So," I continued, "if Jesus is Michael the archangel, why does the Father say he's never called an angel a son? Why has he never told an angel that he's begotten him? Over and over again, the Bible refers to Jesus as 'the only begotten Son.' So how do you explain that?" But I didn't want him to explain. I wanted him to become mute so I could win this round.

So I didn't wait for him to respond. "Also, why are all the angels in heaven worshiping Jesus when worship in heaven is reserved for God? And why does the Father say that Jesus' throne is forever and ever, when we know that only God's throne is forever and ever? Explain that to me, John."

Truth be told, I had gotten pretty aggressive and loud, and if I'm being completely honest, a little condescending. But, man, the dude had it coming. He had been making me look like a fool for weeks, and I was sick of it.

John just glared at me, simmering, while I stood there with my Bible spread open. For the first time he looked unsure of himself—misplaced even, like a run-on sentence searching for its voice in the middle of the page. John's confidence left and traveled somewhere distant, and my confidence swelled into a victory song inside me. John told me he'd study the passage and get back to me.

Man, I loved it. Watching him tap out like that—with everyone watching—was like the apologetics equivalent of a knockout. All my friends looked so proud. Their claps and smiles lifted me up and carried me across the room. I had definitely redeemed myself in the eyes of my friends and about a half a dozen onlookers.

"There you go, Preston!" Brittany all but cackled. "You brought the fire today! I told y'all, this is what Preston does!"

She was right—I did bring the fire.

But she was also dead wrong.

Listen, it's great to be on fire for the Lord. Fire is good. It brings light to dark places. It brings warmth when the crisp breath of night begins to bite at your skin. But if you don't learn how to control it, it can also be destructive. It can spread fast, harming everybody it touches. The same goes for knowledge. Knowing your way around Scripture and being familiar enough with your opponent's arguments to be able to anticipate where they're going and how to counter them can be effective. But if you wield knowledge like a weapon or become more preoccupied with shutting someone down than opening them up to hear what you have to say, it can do more harm than good.

Now, it would have been easy for me to blame John for the way I acted. He made me feel low. He deserved the treatment I gave him, right?

I've been an evangelist and apologist for more than a decade now, and if there's one thing I've learned, it's that people don't make you do anything. They just bring out what's already inside you.

Jesus says, "Out of the abundance of the heart [the] mouth speaks" (Luke 6:45), and man, back then, my mouth told on my heart many days while talking to John.

For weeks, I felt insecure because John knew more Scripture than I did. That wasn't his fault. It was mine for not studying enough. He didn't make me look bad in front of my friends. My lack of knowledge did. John didn't make me prideful. He just brought my insecurity, pride, and wounded ego to the surface. And once my ego got a glimpse of daylight, it became like an unwanted guest in our conversations.

Not only was God using John to reveal something important to me that would shape the way I did apologetics forever, God was exposing my heart as an evangelist. When John's sharp words cut the skin of my pride, I bled so shamelessly in front of people for a reason. I put too much hope in being "Preston the evangelist" at my school, not in Christ and the cross of Calvary alone.

THERE'S A DIFFERENCE BETWEEN DEFENDING YOUR FAITH AND DEFENDING AN IDENTITY THAT YOU PUT TOO MUCH PRIDE IN—AN IDENTITY THAT YOU USE TO HIDE YOUR FAITH BEHIND.

There's a difference between defending your faith and defending an identity that you put too much pride in—an identity that you use to hide your faith behind. It can become so easy for Christians to get caught up in what we do for the Lord, instead of being content in who we are in the Lord.

The Bible says that "knowledge puffs [us] up" and makes us haughty (1 Corinthians 8:1). There's no question it did with me. Every time I backed John into a corner, Brittany, Junior, Dion, and the others would cheer me on, so I studied my tail off, and before I knew it, I got all wrapped up in *what* I knew as opposed to *who* I knew.

My obsession with being "right" and "winning" got in the way of me seeing John as someone who genuinely needed to understand the truth. I wasn't concerned about what was right. I was more focused on who looked right. It reminds me of the political climate we live in. If a candidate can convince you that their opponent isn't credible, that's all they have to do to win many people's votes. It's less about truth than about making the other person look like a liar.

Thank the Lord, Gary was about to set me straight.

Later that afternoon, Gary picked me up at school so we could go hoop, and I could not wait to tell him about how I'd KO'd John. I was so excited. Gary had barely said, "What up, P, how was sch—?" before I blurted out, "Hey, man, I got into another conversation with that Jehovah's Witness today."

"Cool, cool," he said, peeling away from the curb. "That the same dude you been talking to all this time?"

"Yeah, same dude. So we were sitting around the table, and he brought up that whole Jesus is Michael the archangel thing . . ." and I walked that boy through the entire debate, right up to the moment where John gave up. "You should have seen his face, bro!" I laughed. "I'm telling you, dude had nothin' to say!"

I fully expected Gary to be proud, but instead, he kinda side-eyed me and said, "Let me ask you a question, P. Are you still trying to win this cat's heart?"

"Win his heart?" I wasn't even sure what that meant.

"Yeah," Gary said. "'Cause it sounds to me like you're more interested in winning an argument."

This was not the reaction I was expecting at all. "Well . . . yeah. I mean, you said apologetics was about defending your faith."

"Yeah, man, but don't get so caught up in arguing with the dude that you forget why you're trying to witness to him in the first place. Remember, P, the goal isn't to beat him in a fight. It's to win his heart for the Lord. Apologetics ain't about defeating people. It's about reaching them."

It was like the Lord used Gary to snatch the sky from under me. I dropped from cloud nine into a low valley in a matter of seconds. Not only did Gary's rebuke humble me, it also made me think. In all the time we'd spent witnessing on the basketball courts, I'd never once heard him raise his voice, put anyone down, or make a joke at someone else's expense. Gary just met people where they were at, listened to them, and tried to help them understand how knowing the Lord could make their lives better. All I'd done was hurl Scripture at John, insult his religion, and tell him why everything he believed was wrong. At that moment I realized I had strayed away from what Gary had taught me. Just because John was a Jehovah's Witness, it didn't mean I shouldn't care for his soul the way I'd seen Gary care for others. I had no excuse. I felt conflicted. It was like godly conviction and self-condemnation were playing tug-of-war with me.

Gary looked over and saw that his rebuke had fallen on fertile ground. "You all right, bro?"

"Nah . . . yeah. You're right. I'm sorry, man."

"What are you apologizing to me for?"

"I just . . . I thought I was holdin' it down for God's Kingdom. I just thought you would be proud, so your response caught me a little off guard. That's all."

"I *am* proud of you, P," he said as he slapped the back of his hand on my arm. "Man, you've been devouring Scripture these past few months. And I love that you're truly invested in this dude. What's his name again?"

"John."

"John what?"

I froze. I had no idea. "I don't know."

"That's all right. That's all right," Gary said reassuringly. "Has he always been a Jehovah's Witness? Is it like a family thing with him, or did he come into it later?"

Aw, man . . . "I don't know."

Gary just nodded his head. "You ever share your story with him?"

"Nah. We never really talk, you know? We pretty much just debate Scripture." I felt terrible. Here I'd been facing off against this dude for almost four months now, and I didn't know anything about him other than that he was a Jehovah's Witness. I didn't even know the dude's last name! I turned and looked out the window so Gary wouldn't see how conviction was swallowing me whole. "Gary, I'm really sorry, bro. You're right. I know you're right. The guy was just coming after the Lord so hard. He was spewing all kinds of blasphemous stuff—and in front of a bunch of other people too. I was just trying to defend the faith like 1 Peter says, remember?"

"I hear you, P. But listen up, bro," Gary said. "I want you to do me a favor."

"Yeah, sure." Whatever it was, at this point, it felt like the least I could do.

"When you get home tonight, I want you to take a closer look at 1 Peter 3:15."

"About defending your faith?"

"Yeah," he said, easing his Mustang into an open spot right across from the park. "That's the one."

"Why?"

He reached back, grabbed his basketball off the back seat, and pushed the door open with his foot. Then he smiled and said, "Just read it, Preston, and tell me what you think."

That night, I took a closer look at 1 Peter 3:15. The first part was very familiar: "In your hearts honor Christ the Lord as holy, always being prepared to make a defense to anyone who asks you for a reason for the hope that is in you."

There was no doubt in my mind that Christ the Lord was holy. He had changed my entire life, and I knew in my heart that he is who he said he is. And I definitely had the defense part down. I had spent countless hours studying. Nobody was more prepared than I was.

Then I read on: "Yet do it with gentleness and respect, having a good conscience, so that, when you are slandered, those who revile your good behavior in Christ may be put to shame."

Whoa.

I had completely missed the gentleness and respect part. If anything, I had done the exact opposite. I mean, dang. One of the first things I ever said to John was "I think you're in a cult, bro." No wonder it seemed like the dude didn't like me. And since talking with Gary that afternoon, I definitely did not have a good conscience about how I'd handled things with him. In fact, now that I thought about it, my behavior was about as far from good or Christlike as you could get—especially during today's debate. I grabbed my highlighter and went over it again.

Man, there ain't even a period between "the hope that is in you" and "do it with gentleness and respect." It's all one big thought. How could I have missed that?

Gary was right. I needed to spend time thinking about all of this.

All right, so . . . let's look at this text a little closer together.

Peter is writing to Gentiles (non-Jews) who are being persecuted for their faith, and in this part of the letter, he is reminding them of the powerful witness that comes through suffering. After all, you see someone who seems happy in spite

MAN, THERE AIN'T
EVEN A PERIOD
BETWEEN "MAKE
A DEFENSE . . .
FOR THE HOPE
THAT IS IN YOU"
AND "DO IT WITH
GENTLENESS AND
RESPECT." IT'S ALL
ONE BIG THOUGHT.
HOW COULD I HAVE
MISSED THAT?

of horrendous circumstances, you kinda wanna know why, right? That's what Peter means when he says to be "prepared to make a defense for the hope that is in you." It's not so much a defense like somebody is coming after you and you have to fight back. It's more of a reason, an explanation. "How can you be so hopeful? I mean, look around. There's poverty, crime, sickness, hatred, war, death, destruction. Man, what do you know that I don't?" Peter's posture here isn't combative. It's instructive. He's not saying, "Take 'em down." He's saying, "Help people understand why you are so hopeful. Share the Good News."

In fact, before he even gets into that, he tells them,

> Have unity of mind, sympathy, brotherly love, a tender heart, and a humble mind. Do not repay evil for evil or reviling for reviling, but on the contrary, bless, for to this you were called, that you may obtain a blessing.
> I PETER 3:8-9

That's the posture Peter wants us to have when sharing our faith with others—one of humility, kindness, and love.

He then goes on to say, "But in your hearts, honor Christ the Lord as holy." So right from the jump, he makes it clear that apologetics is not an intellectual pursuit; it's a heart issue. I think that when most people think of apologetics, the first word that comes to mind is *knowledge*. We think we need to know the Bible inside and out and be ready to present an airtight defense that immediately shuts down our opponent so we can win an argument. I know I did. But what if the first word that came to mind when we thought about apologetics was *love*?

Think about it. Jesus didn't just present facts. He asked questions. He told stories. He didn't focus on information. He focused on people. He spent time with them. He talked with them. He prayed with them. He ate with them. Most importantly, he *loved* them. And he loved them well.

Peter knew this. He was there when Jesus washed his feet and gave the disciples the command to "love one another: just as I have loved you, you also are to love one another. By this all people will know that you are my disciples, if you have love for one another" (John 13:34-35). That's why he opens with love. Then he tells us to be ready to give a defense—or to explain—why we have hope. And then he says, "Yet do it with gentleness and respect" (1 Peter 3:15). You see what he did there? He opened with the heart and then closed with conduct. Why? Because how we talk to people matters to God. How we treat people matters to God. How we conduct ourselves matters to God. Yes, the words we use matter, but God uses our words best when we present them with love.

THE GOSPEL IS THE GREATEST GIFT WE CAN GIVE TO THE WORLD. THIS IS WHY THE LORD CARES HOW WE DELIVER IT.

As Christians, we can often believe the world is rejecting the truth we speak. But what if that's not always the case? If you give someone a gift that's in a garbage bag, they might not be rejecting the gift but the way you gave it to them. The gospel is the greatest gift we can give to the world. This is why the Lord cares how we deliver it. The first time I shared the truth with John, I gave it to him in a garbage bag. John didn't merely reject the truth I gave. He rejected me. And he should have. I came to school seeking to give him God's Word but left my good conduct at home.

But Peter still isn't finished. He goes on to say that we should share the reason for our hope with gentleness and respect, "having a good conscience, so that, when you are slandered, those who revile your good behavior in Christ may be put to shame" (1 Peter 3:16).

The reason Peter urges us to make sure we walk away from sharing our faith with a good conscience is because even if we give a great defense, if we don't deliver it with gentleness and respect, our behavior can negate any positive effect our message might have had.

For example, a few years ago, I was out in Little Five Points near where I live in Atlanta with a couple friends from church, and we were talking with some Hebrew Israelites who were out preaching on the corner. The conversation started off great, but once they realized we were Christians, man, those dudes got hostile. Next thing I knew, they were yelling stuff like "You all believe in the white man's religion! You've been brainwashed! You're a victim of your slave masters' teachings!" And I'm telling you, these dudes got loud.

Here's the thing, though. It wasn't just us standing there. There were a bunch of other people standing around listening, and at one point, one of the dudes listening in nodded towards me and my friends and said, "Man, I don't know which one of y'all is right, but I'd rather believe in your God, brother, because these dudes are treating y'all like trash!"

The way we represent Christ matters. We should never walk away from a conversation confident that we told the truth but not confident in *how* we told that truth. The truth of the gospel is offensive enough. We don't have to add to the offense with our bad conduct. In other words, don't let your pride murder your message.

The bottom line is this: the way we do apologetics looks different when we are motivated not by our desire to conquer the other person but by our genuine love and compassion and by our desire to see people discover God's life-giving truth.

> **THE WAY WE REPRESENT CHRIST MATTERS. WE SHOULD NEVER WALK AWAY FROM A CONVERSATION CONFIDENT THAT WE TOLD THE TRUTH BUT NOT CONFIDENT IN *HOW* WE TOLD THAT TRUTH.**

What Gary wanted me to understand—and what I very much needed to learn—was that apologetics isn't about winning a debate. True apologetics is about honoring Christ as holy, loving others more than ourselves, and presenting the gospel of Jesus Christ in love.

I spent a lot of time over the next week thinking about John, and the more I thought about him, the more I developed a heart not for defeating him but for reaching him. And in order to do that, I realized I didn't just need to learn more about Scripture; I needed to learn more about *him*. Now, don't hear me say that I wasn't still committed to learning the Scriptures. Learning truthful information is vital when trying to reach a world dying of lies. I just didn't want to find my identity in the information. When we find our identity in the *information* we know instead of the *God* we know, we'll treat people like projects and not image bearers. By this point, I was fully convinced that the way I'd approached John wasn't pleasing to God.

The following week, when I got to the cafeteria, John was sitting at our usual table, Bible in hand, waiting for me. I had deliberately shown up a little late. I'm not going to lie, I was nervous, and a big part of me wanted to avoid him. It's a vulnerable thing to approach someone after God tapped you on the wrist and told you that you were wrong.

"Hey, man," I said, sitting down across from him. I could tell by the look in John's eyes he was ready for another war. "I've been doing a lot of thinking these past few days, and the thing is, I'm tired of just arguing with you all the time."

He looked at me with distrust, like I had a knife behind my back. "What . . . you mean you don't want to talk anymore?"

"No, man, no," I explained. "I like talking with you. I just . . . we've been doing this for almost four months now, and . . . I mean, I don't know anything about you."

Dude looked at me like I'd just suggested we go bike riding together or something. It was awkward, but I was convinced it was necessary.

"I just don't want to try to prove you wrong every day, is all." He didn't seem to know what to do with that, so I kept going. "Let me ask you a question." Instinctively, he sat up a little straighter and rested his hand on his Bible. Being war ready is all he knew with me. "How did you first become a Jehovah's Witness?" I asked.

He cocked his head to the side a little. "Seriously?"

"Yeah. I really wanna know."

He sat back, stared at me a second, then launched into his story. He didn't go into a lot of details, but what he did tell me spoke volumes. It turns out, when he was little, he and his mom both attended a Christian church. But then she started noticing a lot of things happening at the church that bothered her and made her question her faith. Right around that same time, she started talking to some Jehovah's Witnesses, and a few months later, she joined them and brought John along with her.

"So it didn't have anything to do with God or Jesus?" I asked. "It was just a lot of bad stuff happening within the church?"

He thought about that for a second. "Yeah."

But then, he told me, a few years ago, his mom met some Christians, and she started going to their church, which made her question a lot of what the Jehovah's Witnesses believed, and when the Witnesses found out about it, she was excommunicated. I couldn't help but think, *What was her encounter with those Christians like? How were they able to impact her in a way that made her return to a faith that had failed her in the past?* He never told me, but I bet you it had something to do with her feeling loved.

"Wow, man, excommunicated," I said. "That's pretty intense. Do you and your mom ever talk about your faith?"

He just shook his head. "Nah, man. We're not really on speaking terms."

I began to understand why he went so hard against Christianity. In his eyes, Christians took his mother away. His pain was deeper than our disagreements about Jesus.

"Dude, I'm so sorry." I asked him how he dealt with it, and he said he missed her, but ultimately, he trusts God with her life. For a moment his eyes drifted away from our conversation, and he stared off into the distance, as if he could see the mother he could no longer talk to. I almost wanted to hug the dude. It was wild. He wasn't a Jehovah's Witness who didn't believe Jesus was God—he was just a guy who was hurting because his family had been ripped apart by the church. He was a son longing for his mother.

I could relate to him. The Christian church should be a safe place for all. But churches are often run by wounded people who wound others.

Growing up, my mother didn't take me to church often, but most of the churches she did take me to rubbed me the wrong way. Once when I was around thirteen, my mom took me to this Pentecostal church. I didn't understand it at all. This is no shade. I've met faithful Pentecostals since then. But back then, I was deeply wounded by the church we attended.

I wasn't what you'd call a model child. I'd already had a few run-ins with the law, and I was always in some kind of trouble at school, so at one point in the service, my mom brought me up to the altar so the preacher could "lay hands on me" or, I don't know, knock the devil out of me or something. There were four or five other teenagers up there with me, and one at a time, the preacher would put his hands on their shoulders, close his eyes, and shout something about the devil needing to leave them. Then he'd push them backwards a little bit until they fell onto the floor—healed, I suppose.

When he got to me, he put his hands on my shoulders, closed his eyes, and shouted, "I pray that the enemy releases his grip on you!" Then he pushed me, and I thought, *Why did this man just push me?* I clenched my core tight and straightened my back stiffly and refused to go down. He did it again, and this time he pushed really hard, almost like he was *trying* to knock me down. But yet again my body was stubborn and wasn't about to play his game. After the second push, the look I gave him told him not to touch me again. I don't know if he really thought I had a demon or if he thought I was just some bad kid. I just know I didn't feel loved. "Sometimes the demons really take hold of a young soul," he said to the congregation. "Let's all join together and pray for life over this young man!" Then he prayed, smiled empathetically at my mother, gave me the stink eye, and told us to go back to our seats.

Now, I'm not saying all that falling stuff is fake. I believe some people really do have sincere encounters with God in ways we can't always explain. But between you and me, I still think those other kids were pretending to fall because they knew they were supposed to. I was just too rebellious to play games in church. But looking back, I can see that was the first time the church wounded me, embarrassing me by trying to pray a demon out of me that I don't believe was there.

For the first time since we'd met, I realized that John's anger wasn't directed so much at me as it was directed at the Christian church. I just happened to be a representative.

Now that I finally understood where he was coming from, I knew how I could best minister to him. "Hey, man, I'm so sorry for all the pain the church has caused you. I get that." Then, just to break the tension a little, I told him about my Pentecostal experience. We both had a good laugh, and it felt like his guard dropped a little. "Not all Christian churches are bad, though," I cautioned him. "Writing off all of them because of one bad experience is like writing off all white people just because you ran into one white dude you didn't particularly like. All people are flawed, man. That's why we all need a Savior, you feel me?"

"I feel you," he said. Then he looked at me quizzically and said, "So, what about you? How'd you go from refusing to fall at the crazy man's church to arguing with me all the time about Jesus?"

So I told him about growing up in the hood, hearing the gospel for the first time in my girlfriend's living room, the day my friend got shot, going to live with my aunt Denise, meeting Gary, the girl at the bank, and the night I accepted Christ in my room. By the time I was finished, he seemed almost as taken aback by my story as I was by his.

He'd just assumed I'd been raised in the church. But hearing about how Jesus had slowly softened my heart and how God had called me into his family forced him to reframe some of his preconceived notions—if not about Christians in general, at least about me.

"Man, Christians always struck me as being kinda lazy, you know?" he said. "You're the first one I've met that actually studies Scripture."

"Aw . . . dude, there are a whole bunch of Christians who study like me. Not every Christian is like the people you and your mom met early on."

We talked for the better part of an hour. I told him about my grandmother and my aunt and what amazing prayer warriors they both were. And, of course, I told him about how Gary and I would go down to Washington Park, play basketball, and talk to others about our faith. Shoot, I even told him about how Gary set me straight on 1 Peter 3:15. John got a real kick out of that. And by the time we had to take off for class, we'd both apologized for the way we'd treated one another.

We still met at lunch twice a week to talk about God, faith, and the Bible, and every once in a while, we would even break out in a debate. But it was much more lighthearted. We didn't butt heads as much, and even when we disagreed, our friendship kept our egos and tempers in check, and we each made more of an effort to understand where the other was coming from.

For example, instead of just shutting me down or deflecting when I tried to explain why the Trinity was so important, John would hear me out, ask for some passages he could study on his own, and say, "Okay, P, I'll consider that." And I became a much better listener. Before, I had been so determined to prove John wrong that I would usually start formulating my rebuttal in my head before he'd even finished talking. Now, I focused more on understanding why he believed what he believed, and my questions became less accusatory and more inquisitive—more personal. Sometimes we didn't talk about Scripture at all. We'd just talk about our families, classes, movies—whatever happened to come up. And the more I got to know John, the less I saw him as an opponent—or even a Jehovah's Witness—and the more I began to see him as a friend and fellow image bearer. I no longer wanted to defeat him. I genuinely wanted to reach him, to help him see the Lord in a different light, and to understand that salvation is not just reserved for a select few but is there for the taking for anyone who truly wants it.

Funny thing is, as soon as we stopped debating, the crowds disappeared. Every once in a while, Brittany or Dion or Junior would come sit with us for a little bit, but now that the fireworks were over, they lost interest. So, most days, it was just me and John—no posturing, no mocking, no shouting—just two dudes sitting around talking about why they loved the Lord, even if we didn't always agree on who the Lord was.

John eventually moved to another city, and we lost touch. But ever since then, I've tried my best to keep the same "heart-focused" approach when talking to others that I learned through our time together. I don't know where he is now or if he still holds the same beliefs he had when we were in college. I just hope that if and when he thinks of me, he remembers that I was a Christian that loved him.

If we think of apologetics solely in terms of debate and argument—as a battle we have to win—we're missing the mark. Yes, we need to be able to present cold, hard truths, and even though some of them may be difficult to hear, we can't compromise on that. Nor can we let our guard down and stop studying Scripture. But we also need to remember that when all is said and done, the main goal is to reach, not to defeat. Apologetics is about defending Scriptural truths, but it's also about loving people more than knowledge. And it's about correcting people's false narratives about Jesus in a way that is not only truthful but that also represents him well.

Since those days of arguing with John, I've learned a lot about how to lovingly and effectively defend my faith—much of it by trial and error—and now I'd like to pass some of those practical strategies along to you. But I'm telling you, if you take nothing else away from this book, please, let it be this: the ultimate goal of apologetics is not to win an argument—it is to win a heart.

5

LEARNING FROM
THE MASTER

Up to this point, we've been focusing pretty heavily on how to prepare for evangelism—knowing the person you're talking to and entering into the conversation to win their heart, not just the argument. We've also talked about what to share—who Jesus is and how to be saved. Well, now it's time to talk about how to share, because the gospel is a powerful, life-changing message, a precious gift given to us to give to others. With wisdom and the right methods, we can use this gift to persuade others to stop feasting with the world and invite them to come dine with Jesus forever. But if you can remember from the last chapter, if we serve the gospel up on a garbage can lid, instead of on a dignifying platter, we give people an excuse to reject it. You feel me?

I mean, if someone chooses to reject Christ's message and the beauty of his blood poured out for them when it is given with respect—we can lift up clean hands before God and beg him to remember mercy for their rebellious soul. But if they reject his message because we were offensive in the way we presented it—let us ask God to kill our pride and all the other sin inside us that might be in the way of the gospel. We don't ever want our personal conduct or behavior to be the reason someone rejects the gospel. Granted, presenting the gospel without insulting someone is one thing; loving them calmly and getting them to lower their guard is another. That's where soft skills come into play.

When Jesus sent his disciples out to preach, he told them, "Be wise as serpents and innocent as doves" (Matthew 10:16). A serpent is patient. It lies and waits, statue-still, until it's the right time to strike. It is hard to speed it up. It slithers the earth at its own pace, minimizing its chances for mistakes. A serpent is never seen until it wants to be. It spends more time watching its prey in the shadows than giving all its energy away hunting in the sun. And doves—doves are gentle. Not only will they not harm you, but it is not even in their nature to do so. Their motives are as pure as the white feathers that blanket their bodies. If you violently handle a dove, it doesn't even think to fight back but naturally humbles itself to others, making itself easy to deal with.

Are we patient like serpents? Do we spend enough time watching our community, praying for the right time to strike with the gospel? Or do we hunt more than we watch and pray, and talk more than we listen? And when we talk to others, do we wisely guide the conversation, stirring it to where we want it to go? Or do we allow them to set the pace of the conversation, taking us down rabbit holes that lead nowhere? And are we gentle like doves? Are any of the bones inside us still malicious, or do we engage with people with a new nature? And even so, will our motives remain pure as doves even if the people we're trying to reach don't handle us with care?

Lastly, the thing these two creatures have in common is that they are both quiet. A serpent is quiet because wisdom tells it that being heard at the right time will help it be more successful in life. It only makes noise when it has to. A dove is quiet because their very nature is soft, not hardened by the cruel world around them. Unlike these creatures, we often let the world and social media disciple us *loud*. We can spend more time yelling at the world and shouting with our fingers in comment sections online than trying to figure out how to engage with the world with wisdom.

Jesus was telling his disciples that they should go into these situations with their eyes wide open, discerning the best way to say what needed to be said. They needed to be wise to recognize the opportunities that would be open to them as they went out. And because they went as his representatives, they also needed to be gentle and loving so they could make him look like the good God that he is. And that's what Jesus' disciples still need today.

For the first four months I was witnessing to John, I was a sledgehammer instead of a dove. But in God's divine guidance, right after I left vocational college, I took a job selling home security systems door-to-door, and let me tell you, man did that help me to develop my soft skills.

It's cool, you can laugh at me, but being a door-to-door salesman isn't all that different from being an evangelist. In both cases, you're trying to win someone's trust and then keep them engaged long enough for you to tell them everything they need to hear in order to make a decision. And being polite and personable is vital. Without it, our evangelism has little chance for survival.

Granted, I'm an extrovert, and I genuinely enjoy meeting and talking with people, so encouraging soft skills can sound like I'm trying to make everyone just like me. But the truth is that even if you're an introvert, no matter who you are, there are things you can do—like smiling, making eye contact, maintaining a warm and friendly tone, not interrupting, and taking the time to learn and call people by their first name—that can go a long, long way towards making other people want to hear what you have to say.

When I sold security systems, for example, I never opened with, "Hi, I'm selling security systems," because that would give people the option of saying they're not interested and slamming the door closed. And the key to success in sales—and in sharing our faith with others—is the ability to draw people into a conversation. So instead of telling people I was selling alarm systems, I would instead ask them a question like "Have you heard about the break-ins in the neighborhood lately?" Instead of telling someone I would like to talk to them about

God, I would instead ask questions like "What do you think about God?" or "Who is Jesus to you?" Not only do questions like this help eliminate a chance for them to reject you, but it gives them a chance to be heard. And if there's one thing I've learned engaging with others, it's that every heart has a cry. Some cries are louder than others, but every cry wants to be heard. Being invested and truly hearing people will only help us in our evangelism. If you ask the right questions and listen with pure motives, people will teach you how to best serve them.

One time when I knocked on a door, a sweet, elderly, coffee-colored woman opened it. Her hair was a gray sky of wisdom, and her smile said welcome. The first question I asked her was "Have you heard about the break-ins in the area?" She folded her wrist and put it on her hips, gathered up all her concern and placed it in her eyes, looked at me, and said, "Have I!"

"Tell me about it," I said.

Boy, did she take me down memory lane. She told how she watched her neighborhood through the years turn from safe to a war zone, how in the '80s the only thing she saw fly on her street was birds, but all she sees now are bullets. She told me about a time everybody on the block could leave their doors unlocked and wide open in early spring and cool autumn to keep the air-conditioning bill low. "Not any more," she said, waving her head like a red flag. She was done and fed up with what her neighborhood had become. "If I had the money and wasn't on a fixed income, I would've moved to the north side a long time ago." She said sometimes she feels like she's just waiting her turn for somebody to break into her house. "But the good Lord has kept me!"

"Are you a Christian?" I asked.

"Yes, I am. I've been saved for thirty-four years!"

"I am too," I told her. "I've been a Christian for a little over a year." We really hit it off after that. We talked about the Lord and how I came to faith. And by the time I left, I had sold her her first alarm system.

I want to make sure I make this clear, because I know salesmen can often be seen as untrustworthy people. Well, unfortunately, so can Christians. When I built trust with this sweet lady, I made sure I didn't take advantage of her. I could have upsold her to make a bigger sale. But instead, I sold her what I felt like she needed, nothing more and nothing less. Evangelism is a lot similar. There is nothing immoral about asking people questions in order to figure out how to best give them the free gift of the gospel, just as long as we try our best to discern what they need. Just as long as we have pure motives.

GENERALLY SPEAKING, PEOPLE DON'T LIKE TO FEEL LIKE THEY'RE BEING LECTURED. THEY DO, HOWEVER, LIKE TO BE HEARD.

That's why Gary would always talk to the dudes on the basketball court about the problems in the hood. For one thing, it showed them that he was aware of the issues they were dealing with. It also gave them an opportunity to vent some of their own frustrations and to share their theories about why things were so messed up. By the time Gary started talking about sin and redemption, they were fully engaged. Now, if he had just walked onto the court and said, "Hey, man, I'm here to tell y'all about Jesus," those dudes would have been like *Here goes another weirdo talking at us*, because generally speaking, people don't like to feel like they're being lectured. They do, however, like to be heard. As my grandmother always used to say, "Preston, there's a reason God gave you two ears but only one mouth. It's so you can listen twice as much as you speak." Thank God for the wisdom that flows from our elders that's plain but yet ocean deep.

Soft skills are an important tool in any evangelist's toolbox. And while I learned a lot about how to interact with people in my time as a salesman, if I'm being completely honest, I didn't come up with them myself—I just followed the Master.

Jesus was the master at drawing people into conversation—of noticing, intriguing, and challenging people. There's a reason people invited him to parties and wanted to be around him. And there's a reason, too, why proselytizing today is so often seen as a four-letter word. Too often those who claim to represent Christ engage others in a way that betrays the Jesus they claim to represent. So let's try to learn some of the "soft skills" we need to effectively share our faith from the one who did it best.

One of my favorite stories in the Bible is in John 9, when Jesus heals a man that's been blind since birth. But the thing I love about the story the most is how it starts off. "As [Jesus]

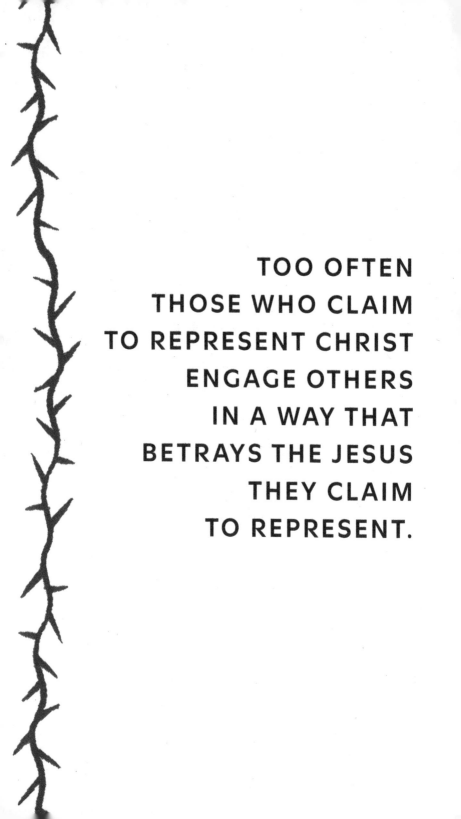

TOO OFTEN
THOSE WHO CLAIM
TO REPRESENT CHRIST
ENGAGE OTHERS
IN A WAY THAT
BETRAYS THE JESUS
THEY CLAIM
TO REPRESENT.

passed by, he saw a man blind from birth" (John 9:1). Notice how this story doesn't start off with Jesus healing a blind man; it starts off with Jesus *seeing* a blind man. In the same way, our evangelism should start with us seeing people. Seeing needs. Seeing stories. Seeing thirsty people who need a drink of everlasting water. In the very first chapter of Mark, we are told that "after John [the Baptist] was arrested, Jesus came into Galilee, proclaiming the gospel of God, and saying, 'The time is fulfilled, and the kingdom of God is at hand; repent and believe the gospel'" (Mark 1:14-15). Jesus the evangelist here is going around sharing the Good News, and he sees a man who had been born blind. Many people looked at this man every day, but they didn't truly *see* him. Jesus sees this man is in need, and he's moved with compassion to act on his behalf. Jesus spits in the mud, puts the mud in the man's eyes, and tells the man to go wash his eyes out. He obeys and comes back healed. Notice that when Jesus sees him, he isn't moved to first give him a gospel presentation but to meet a need. Jesus eventually *does* offer him life, though, when he offers himself.

Later on in the story the Pharisees come with hearts dark as moonless midnights and kick the once blind man out of the synagogue because he won't speak against Jesus. Jesus returns and finds the man and another miracle happens:

> Jesus heard that they had cast him out, and having found him he said, "Do you believe in the Son of Man?" He answered, "And who is he, sir, that I may believe in him?" Jesus said to him, "You have

seen him, and it is he who is speaking to you." He said, "Lord, I believe," and he worshiped him.

JOHN 9:35-38

Did you see that? Jesus healed this man of physical blindness, but the man still didn't have the spiritual eyes to see that the one who touched him earlier wasn't just a man but God clothed in humanity. So Jesus came back and healed him a second time, but this time of his spiritual blindness. What is my point? Jesus had every intention of revealing himself to the man so the man could do the very thing he was created for— worship God. But Jesus met his physical needs before he met his spiritual ones, because Jesus cares about the whole person. Jesus is God. He doesn't need to serve others first in order to reveal himself to them. He could have easily healed this man of his spiritual blindness first. But Jesus used this to show us how to get a heart ready for him. When the veil was snatched from the man's spiritual eyes, his heart was ready for worship. I can imagine how much he remembered that he couldn't see anything until Jesus lifted the black from his natural eyes. So when Jesus lifted the veil from his spiritual eyes, the man quickly placed his trust in the one who had earned it earlier.

My friends, in the same way, more people will listen to us share Jesus when they can remember how they were hungry before we fed them, how they were naked before we clothed them. In the words of my grandmother, "People don't care what you know until they know that you care." But as important as it is to meet people's physical needs, we can't just leave it there.

I've often heard people quote the line, "Preach the gospel at all times, and if necessary use words," as if to say, "Love people like Jesus with your actions, and only speak the gospel when you have to." That might sound wise and even holy to some on the surface. But when you dig a little, how true is it? Paul says, "How then will they call on him in whom they have not believed? And how are they to believe in him of whom they have never heard? And how are they to hear without someone preaching?" (Romans 10:14). Good deeds without the truth of the gospel will only make us philanthropists. But the truth of the gospel without good deeds will make us look like hypocrites. So I say, serve others well with your actions, so that when you speak the gospel, your words will hit harder!

Let's look at some more details from the story in John 9. It would have been easy to pass by the man born blind, as so many did, but Jesus sees the man, which draws the attention of his disciples. Now, right away, they ask him, "Rabbi, who sinned, this man or his parents, that he was born blind?" (John 9:2). Such an insensitive question, don't you agree? But Jesus responds graciously because even this is discipleship: "It was not that this man sinned, or his parents, but that the works of God might be displayed in him" (John 9:3). The disciples wanted to know the cause of his suffering. Jesus, however, responds not by giving them the *cause* of his suffering but the *purpose* of his suffering. When we don't see that God has a divine purpose for the people he created, our evangelism will lack grace. When Jesus looked at people, he didn't see their sin only but a story. Because he

BECAUSE JESUS SAW PEOPLE NOT AS THEIR SIN BUT AS STORIES, HE ALWAYS MET THEM WITH COMPASSION.

saw people not as their sin but as stories, he always met them with compassion.

Jesus is the best one to look to when learning how to engage the world around us with the gospel. But we can also learn how not to engage with others by looking at the Pharisees.

After Jesus healed the man born blind, the people who had seen the man in the past as a beggar were surprised and took him to the Pharisees. The Pharisees asked him how it happened, and he was like "Jesus healed me." To which they responded, "This man is not from God, for he does not keep the Sabbath" (John 9:16). Once again, here was a miracle made man—he stood before them once blind now seeing everything—and all they could do was think about the law. Isn't this just like the political climate we live in today, when people care more about laws and policies than people and stories? They even asked the man, "What do you say about Jesus, since he opened your eyes?" They weren't curious about Jesus; they just wanted to know where the man stood. Even today, we are often more concerned with where other people stand than with giving them Jesus. When we're more invested in politics than we are in people, when someone shares their story, we won't hear a testimony but a position. We won't hear a cry but a stance. I've learned from Jesus to not just respond to others with what I see on the surface. But to serve others well, I ask them good questions so I can listen carefully for the soft cry beneath the surface.

One day while evangelizing in a community filled with New Age religions and atheists, I started a conversation with a young Black woman. At first glance I could tell she was the eclectic type. Two crystal necklaces hugged her collarbone, familiar, like inseparable old friends. Her black leather jacket was worn down yet riddled with character, like one of those hidden thrift store treasures you find buried at the back of the clothes rack. When I introduced myself as a Christian, her smile furled with intrigue. She reminded me of how most police officers conduct themselves when they pull you over at night—how they're open to talk yet careful and guarded all the same.

"Do you believe in God?" I asked her.

"No, I only worship my ancestors," she replied.

My mind immediately jogged over to all the Scriptures I knew that dealt with ancestral worship. *How can I begin to share God's truth with her?* I wondered, while listening to her explain to me why her ancestors were the only ones who deserved her worship. "Well, the Bible warns us not to worship the dead," I said with calmness stitched to my voice so I wouldn't seem aggressive. "Can I share with you why I think Jesus is a better option?"

"To be honest, no you cannot," she replied. "There isn't anything you can tell me about the Christian God that I don't already know. I grew up in the church. I've tried that religion, and it was not for me!"

Every time I would try to reason with her, she rejected me so quickly, almost as if she anticipated what I was going to say. I was getting nowhere fast. I knew the right Scriptures to quote, but they only seemed to upset her more. She wasn't mean, but she was very sharp.

Through asking her questions, I could tell she had been hurt by the church, and all I was doing was opening old wounds by bringing up Scriptures. So I asked her, "What happened between you and the church?"

She rolled her eyes to the back of her head, as if her sight was reluctant to reach back into her memory to revisit what the church had done to her. She let out a chuckle that seemed impulsive and said, "They told me my molestation was God's will and I had to deal with it, basically."

At that moment my heart couldn't sit comfortable inside of my chest. The pain in her started to reach out for help. I knew her pain wasn't as deep as God's love for her, but I had to figure out how to let her know this truth. I thought to myself, *Preston, meet her with compassion and don't just look past her hurt to give her more Scripture.*

"I'm sorry that happened to you," I said.

Before I could say more, she cut me off. I could tell she didn't want my sympathy. "It's okay," she replied. "But let me ask you. Was it God's will for me to get molested?"

"Excuse me?" I said. I was trying to buy more time to answer her question. It caught me so off guard.

"You heard me," she said. "Was it God's will for me to get molested? Was it God's will for me to not have a good relationship with my mother?"

These were hard questions for me to answer. They weren't hard because I didn't know what to say about the sovereignty of God and how he allows things to happen for his glory. I just felt that at this moment I couldn't only depend on what I knew about God. I needed direct help from the God who knows why everything happened to her. I silently prayed, *Lord, please help me.*

The Lord answered me quickly with words I felt in my spirit: *Share your wife's story with her.*

"No, I'm serious, my sista," I began. "I'm so sorry that happened. I can't relate personally, but my wife has a similar story. She was molested when she was younger as well. During our marriage, I've watched her wrestle with what was done to her, and it has been one of the hardest things I've had to go through." Her hardness began to melt. For the first time she looked at me like a fellow image bearer and not one of those Christians trying to convert her back to the pain that once was.

"I'm sorry to hear that," she said. "I really feel for your wife. I know what that feels like."

"But can I tell you what God did with my wife, though?" I asked. When she said yes, I told her, "God saved my wife and used her story to bless people all over the world. God didn't let any of her pain go to waste. God never promised her that bad things wouldn't happen. But guess what, sis? He was with her through it all. He worked out everything for his glory and her good. Because God is good, he will never let us go through purposeless evil. We see the greatest example of this with Jesus. My wife serves a God who didn't just watch her suffer but who sacrificed himself and suffered as well. The great thing about God that your ancestors can't say is that he's not asking you to suffer alone. All of us will experience some type of suffering living in this evil world. But God entered into human history to share in your suffering. I'm sorry that the church hurt you. But God wants to heal you."

You see, I was able to share the gospel with her by using my wife's story, and she even told me, "I'd love to meet your wife someday." But if I wasn't invested in *her* story, if I didn't ask the right questions, I probably would've spent the whole time arguing Scripture with someone I thought was a very angry woman who worshiped her ancestors. But I didn't spend that time only trying to challenge her beliefs; I tried to understand her story so I could meet a need, so I could love her well.

A lot of people think that being a good apologist means having all the right answers. But as you've seen, it's often even more important to ask the right questions.

Most of the time when I was asking John questions, I was doing it to set him up. I had studied Jehovah's Witnesses enough to know exactly what argument he was going to make, so like a chess master, I would ask him questions that I knew would lead to a spiritual checkmate, where I could shut his argument down. In other words, I was asking him questions to reveal what I already knew. It wasn't until I asked him how he became a Jehovah's Witness that he revealed what I needed to know in order to reach him.

Now, Jesus had a decided advantage when it came to asking

people questions. John writes that Jesus "knew what was in a man" (John 2:25). One could argue that he didn't even need to ask questions. And yet he did.

Jesus often taught in parables—short stories with a spiritual lesson—to question his listeners and force their questions in return. One of Jesus' most famous parables—the Parable of the Good Samaritan—was told in response to a lawyer's question ("And who is my neighbor?") and acted as a question in response: "Which of these three, do you think, proved to be a neighbor to the man who fell among the robbers?" (Luke 10:29, 36). Jesus told the Parable of the Persistent Widow to teach his disciples about prayer, but he ended it with a question: "Nevertheless, when the Son of Man comes, will he find faith on earth?" (Luke 18:8). And the open-ended finale to the Parable of the Prodigal Son—the father's saying, "It was fitting to celebrate and be glad, for this brother was dead, and is alive; he was lost, and is found" (Luke 15:32)—acts as a question to the religious leaders who were grumbling that Jesus "receives sinners and eats with them" (Luke 15:2). These stories and questions forced listeners beyond feeling good about themselves to truly examining their hearts and motives.

Jesus understood the value of asking questions. Asking questions draws people in. It keeps them engaged.

When I was selling security systems, I would ask homeowners questions, even questions that weren't related to security. I'd ask things like "How long have you lived here? What drew you to the neighborhood?" and take note of things like family photos, pets, antiques, or special collections. In other words,

I got to know them and learned what was valuable or important to them. Knowing that there were small children in the house or that they had one of those little doggy doors in the mudroom leading out to the backyard helped me customize my sales pitch specifically to them.

As tempting as it may be to work from a script, when we share our faith, it will be a lot stronger and more effective if we personalize it. Nobody wants to feel like a number or a project. They want to feel special. And they are special, man. As God's image bearers, we all are. God loves each and every one of us for the beautifully flawed, unique individuals that we are. And we are called to love others as he loved us (see John 13:34). That's what evangelism is all about—loving others enough to want for them what we have in Christ.

So questions are a valuable way to engage with people. They give the other person a chance to talk. And when people talk, they reveal what's in their hearts, like what they worry about, what they fear, what they doubt, and what they desire. When we know these things about other people, we can better connect them with the truth of Scripture.

When you truly engage with people, they will teach you how to serve them. For example, some of the hardest people I've tried to share the gospel with are the more aggressive camps of Hebrew Israelites. Some camps can be temperamental. They can be loud. And they can be accusatory. Sometimes when I've tried to go toe to toe with these dudes, man, things went downhill fast. When I would start arguing with them about theology, all they heard was "I'm challenging your identity," and they lashed out even harder. But after speaking with these dudes for a long time, I've come to discover that all that hostility is masking a whole lot of hurt.

One time I was talking with this one guy who was out screaming at people on a street corner, and things were starting to get a little heated, because where these dudes come from, a Black guy who follows "the white man's teaching" is the equivalent of being a tax collector in Jesus' day. In other words, I was seen as betraying my brethren. So to de-escalate things a bit, I asked him how he came to be a Hebrew Israelite. At first, he seemed suspicious—almost like I was sent by the government to spy on him or something. I don't think many people have asked him that question, though. But as soon as I assured him, "I'm only asking because I'm curious. I really want to know your story," the dude opened right up.

He told me that growing up, he hated that Black people were always treated like doormats. "The white man has treated Black people wrong for years," he said. "White people have abused us, raped our women, enslaved us, stolen our heritage, stolen our name. Young man, we're still dealing with it! Look at all this police brutality!" Then one day, he heard someone speaking on a street corner, and it was like a light bulb went on. "Man, it all made sense," he said. "We're the chosen people that the Bible talks about."

I came to see that all that anger was basically a trauma response. People formulate ideologies to deal with pain—to help them make sense of it. In doing this, some people turn away from the gospel. They think, *Man, slavery? Police brutality?*

The KKK? God doesn't care about Black people. Some stop believing in God altogether. And others go to the opposite extreme and say, "Oh, that's why all this is happening! We're God's chosen people! The white people are not going to inherit the Kingdom of God—we are!"

Asking this dude why he believed what he believed brought down the temperature of the conversation because it helped him feel seen; it helped him feel heard. Most people don't take the time to get at the "why" behind the way Hebrew Israelites act, so they just write the whole sect off as crazy. But once you understand where they're coming from, it's easier to minister to them.

For example, on another day I was talking with a Hebrew Israelite, and I could just hear the pain in his voice as he described getting picked on in school by white kids because he had dark skin, coarse hair, and a large, ethnic nose. Then, he told me, he found the Hebrew Israelites, and all of a sudden he felt like he had a purpose and an identity.

I said to him, "Forgive me if I'm misreading you here, but it sounds to me like you're finding your identity more in this ideology than in God himself." He got a little defensive, but looking back, I think that had less to do with my questioning his identity and more to do with my comment hitting a little too close to home.

"I hope I'm not misreading *you*, brother, but I think you're a slave to the white man's teaching," he said.

I didn't get offended. Instead, I just asked him another question. "How so?"

"Look at the history, brotha!" he said. "All they've done is evil, and you trust them with your books, your sermons, your family, and your life! You're still enslaved in your mind."

"Can I ask you a question, bro?" I asked.

"Go ahead," he said, looking frustrated at me.

"Hypothetically speaking, if you took everything that white people did to Black people out of the history of this country, do you still have Hebrew Israelism?"

"What are you talking about, man!" he asked, getting upset.

"All of your proof that Black people are the lost children of Israel rests largely on what white people have done to Black people, not mainly on what *God* has done. I'm not making excuses for the evil done to our people throughout the history of this country. But bro, your teaching involves so much of what white men have done compared to what God has done for Black people. All of your ideologies are centered around the evilness of white men. I ask you this with respect, sir—doesn't that make you more of a slave to the white slave master teachings than I am?"

I can't front y'all. He looked at me like he wanted to take my head off. He called me ignorant and told me to have a nice day. But he didn't have an answer for me. Another thing asking a good question does is it allows people to see their own contradictions without you having to say it.

Not every conversation is going to end well. But I truly believe my words made him see a truth that day—a truth that he let the sins of humans, not the faithfulness of God, form his views.

The point is, when you ask people questions—especially about themselves—it shows that you are invested in them personally, and the walls start to come down. And even if the walls stay up, those questions we ask plant seeds in people's minds. God can do wonders with those seeds.

As important as asking questions is, giving people time and space to think about them can be even more important. The more you come at someone with one question after another, without even waiting for a response, the more it starts to feel like you're backing them into a corner, and nobody likes to feel bullied. If you don't believe me, you might ask a certain Pentecostal preacher who's still wondering why he couldn't push a scrawny thirteen-year-old kid to the ground.

Once I was talking with a gay rights activist named Trevon in Little Five Points. He was raised Baptist, but he bumped into a lot of friction in the church after he came out as gay, so he started practicing Buddhism. As we began to talk, I could tell he was nervous. I wanted to make sure I handled him with care. Gay Black men are not often treated as humans by straight Black men where I'm from. He was a really nice guy—big on tolerance and letting people be whoever they want to be and believe whatever they want to believe. This was problematic, yet understandable given his background. The church he came from only saw his sexual orientation and not all of who he was as a person. I tried my best to follow Jesus and not focus only on parts of him that the people in his life deemed unworthy. All of him needed Jesus. Jesus isn't after sexual sin only; Jesus wants his whole heart. I tried my best to make sure I saw all of him. And I wanted him to know that Jesus wanted all of him. Anyway, in the course of our conversation, I asked him who he believed the true and living God to be. I was fully expecting him to say Buddha, but then the dude threw me a curveball and said he believed that we are all our own god.

Now, old Preston would have gone straight for his neck! But the newer, gentler Preston borrowed from the Master's handbook. I asked a series of questions to get him to see the inherent problem with what he was laying down.

I started by restating what I heard him saying—first, to make sure I was understanding him correctly, and second, to make sure he felt heard. When he agreed that I had accurately summarized what he was saying, I said, "Okay, Trevon, help me understand something. You're a gay rights activist, right? Well, if we are all our own god and we all live according to our own standards, how are you able to argue against the person who believes homosexuality is wrong? I mean, what happens when your worldview bumps into mine and we disagree? If we're both our own god, how do we decide who's right and who's wrong?"

I didn't attack him. I didn't tell him he was wrong. I didn't throw Scripture at him. I simply asked him a question to point out a contradiction in what he said he believed.

And then . . . I waited.

This is important.

Old Preston would have kept on pushing. The Bible,

however, tells us that we are to meditate on "whatever is true" (Philippians 4:8), and it's hard to meditate when someone loves the sound of their own voice more than hearing responses to questions. It's a common condition among evangelists—we tend to fall in love with the sound of our own voices and just talk, talk, talk, talk, talk. Problem is, when we do that, we don't allow the other person to really wrestle with the questions we're asking. And in Trevon's case, I wanted him to sit with the contradiction for a bit and really think about it.

You gotta be patient. You gotta have discipline. Because it can be so tempting to jump back in and start connecting the dots for them. Some stuff, though, people need to figure out for themselves, because that's what makes it stick.

That's another reason why Jesus spoke in parables. He knew what he was saying was important. He also knew that a lot of people wouldn't understand what he was laying down. And that was the point. He wanted people to wrestle with his words. His words are life. If we can get people to wrestle with Jesus' words, they might just gain it. He wanted them to think it through, to meditate on it, and to come to their own understanding. Mind you, he did this knowing full well that some people would never understand. He wasn't hiding the truth from anyone. He just knew that the hearts of some people would always be hardened to the truth.

You can feel when a conversation's not going anywhere. If a person's eyes are in the sky instead of making eye contact, or they start scrolling through their phone, it's a pretty good sign they've reached their limit. And that's not necessarily a bad thing. They might just be wrestling with the fact that something you've said has made them uncomfortable or that you've made them question their worldview.

When that happens, I usually just thank them for their time and tell them I enjoyed speaking with them and that I hope they'll continue to think about what we talked about. Sometimes I'll even give them my cell number and extend an invitation to talk more later if they'd like.

In Trevon's case, I could tell he was really wrestling with what I had said, in part because he admitted, "I never thought about it like that before." And then he kept on thinking. And I let him. Finally, after a few minutes, he shook his head, looked at me and said, "I guess I don't really have an answer for that question."

Again, I didn't pounce on homie. I did, however, challenge him to read the Bible and even offered to text him some specific Scriptures to meditate on if he wanted. I quickly shared the gospel with him and thanked him for taking the time to talk to me and wished him all the best. Cool thing is, I could tell when I walked away that the dude had been shaken a little. He was still smiling, but there was an uncertainty there that wasn't apparent when we started talking. I don't know if he ever fully came around to what I was saying, but I do believe I got him to question the validity of some of his own beliefs, and sometimes that's all we can do. Sometimes silence speaks for us. In fact, sometimes the best way we can minister to people is by not saying anything at all.

You want to know one of the most amazing things Jesus ever did—in my opinion? He wept. When his friend Lazarus died, Jesus wept. We know this. We've heard quotes in sermons all our lives. But think about it. Jesus knew that he could—and, in fact, would—raise Lazarus from the dead. So why did he cry? He did so because he knew how to be present. His emotions weren't absent in his ministry.

The Bible says Jesus loved Lazarus. And yet when Lazarus's sisters, Mary and Martha, sent word to Jesus that their brother was sick, he did not come right away. In fact, he stayed away for two more days. Then, when he finally did arrive on the scene, Martha met him mourning. "Lord," she said, "if you had been here, my brother would not have died." She went on, "But even now I know that whatever you ask from God, God will give you" (John 11:21-22). Martha wanted to talk, and Jesus revealed something about himself to her: "I am the resurrection and the life. Whoever believes in me, though he die, yet shall he live, and everyone who lives and believes in me shall never die" (John 11:25-26). Jesus hugged her with his words.

But then Mary met him weeping. Just like Martha, she said, "Lord, if you had been here, my brother would not have died" (John 11:32). But that was it.

Now, he could have started right in preaching. "Don't worry, Mary. I'm about to raise Lazarus from the dead and turn everybody's mourning into a celebration." Or he could have challenged her by saying something like "You know who I am. Why do you doubt me?" But he didn't. He just sat with Mary and wept. He knew everything was going to be okay—that Lazarus would be raised and that Mary and Martha's sorrow would fade and that their joy would return soon. But he didn't act right away—even then. Instead, he chose to be present for a moment with those he loved in their sorrow.

There is something so powerful about sitting with somebody when they're upset or they're mourning, but it's also difficult. Generally speaking, we don't like vulnerability. It's easier to debate information than it is to sit in the uncomfortableness of pain with someone. But isn't that also ministry? Just as the Bible tells us to give the truth of the gospel, it also tells us to bear one another's burdens and to mourn with those who mourn (see Galatians 6:2; Romans 12:15).

Jesus was great at empathy. He wore it like a warm quilt. He knew what to say. He knew what not to say. And he knew when the people he loved would be best served by saying nothing at all.

Sometimes there is nothing to say. Jesus sitting with Mary and weeping is a great reminder that God is not always calling us to speak. Sometimes he wants our tears to communicate.

Over the years, I've learned to be a better listener, and I don't just mean listening to respond. I've become better at listening to understand. When we listen simply to respond, we're not truly listening. More often than not, we're busy formulating our next point in our head while the other person is talking. The truth is, we will serve people better if we take the time to listen—not just to their words but to their hearts.

A few years ago, I saw a video online of an apologist who was standing outside a Planned Parenthood clinic giving the gospel to women who were going in, presumably possibly to have an abortion. Most of them were just ignoring him, but one woman stopped and said, "So you'll know, I was raped. Do you still think I should not be allowed to have an abortion?"

And he said, "Just because somebody raped you doesn't mean you should be able to kill an innocent baby."

Man, I was like "Whoa, fam! You didn't even acknowledge the fact that she said she was raped!"

I don't think he meant harm, but man, his approach was dead wrong. Sadly, it's become such a badge of honor to fight for the unborn in certain evangelical circles that sometimes we forget we're also supposed to care about the mothers. That doesn't mean we have to compromise our values. We can still be bold and honest while at the same time being compassionate and empathetic. Look at the way Jesus interacted with the woman at the well in John 4. He knew she'd had five husbands and that she wasn't married to the man she was currently living with—and he told her as much. But he didn't harp on it or make her feel guilty about it. He simply acknowledged her situation and then offered her a better alternative. Sharing the gospel isn't about making others feel bad about their past. It's about helping them see a more hopeful future in Christ.

SHARING THE GOSPEL ISN'T ABOUT MAKING OTHERS FEEL BAD ABOUT THEIR PAST. IT'S ABOUT HELPING THEM SEE A MORE HOPEFUL FUTURE IN CHRIST.

Bottom line, when we're sharing our faith with others, what we say is important, but how we say it is equally if not even more important. Again, as Jesus' disciples, we are to be "wise as serpents and innocent as doves" (Matthew 10:16). In other words, we need to strike a balance between wisdom and vulnerability, knowledge and heart.

Now, a lot of the examples I have given thus far have involved defending your faith against people of other faiths. Those can be tough conversations to have because they often require knowing enough about the theology of Jehovah's Witnesses, Mormons, Hebrew Israelites, Muslims, or Buddhists to understand how and why their belief systems clash with Christianity.

The soft skills? Those are relevant regardless. It doesn't matter who you're talking to, you always want to be polite, personable, empathetic, and engaging. Even if you know you're never going to see these people again, you want to make a good impression—you want to represent Christ well. There's a famous old saying that goes "Be mindful of how you act and what you say; you may be the only Bible someone ever reads." Man, amen to that.

Here's the thing. Because I have lived most of my life in urban areas that tend to be melting pots for a variety of different religions, I have had literally hundreds of conversations like the ones I've shared thus far, and all of them have presented their own unique challenges. I'll tell you this, though: some of the hardest, most emotionally fraught conversations about faith I've ever had have taken place not on street corners with complete strangers, but in my own living room with friends and family.

So now that you've seen what apologetics looks like out in the wild, it's time to talk about what it looks like to share your faith in your own backyard.

6

TOO CLOSE TO HOME

BECAUSE OF THE SOVEREIGNTY OF GOD and how God has made me, I have no problem asking strangers about who they believe Jesus to be. I've even looked for people of other faiths on the street to talk with them about God and the Bible. But when it comes to talking to my family about faith? I've had my challenges.

The thing is, there's an anonymity that comes with doing evangelism and apologetics with the world around you and not the world you came from. A world that doesn't know anything personal about you. They don't know about the things you fear. They don't know your failures and the ways those failures have attempted to claim you and call you their own. When you share the truth with strangers, it's sometimes easier to be bold because you can hide in plain sight. If strangers get frustrated with you, things turn south, or, God forbid, you lose your cool and fumble a soul or two, odds are you're never going to see those people again anyway. But there's no avoiding family and friends. When telling the truth of the gospel to people who know you, sometimes that familiarity can make talking about your faith a little awkward.

I remember the first family reunion I went to after I became a Christian. Now you gotta remember, I was wild and unruly before I gave my life to Christ. I used to smoke so much weed, my body had become unfamiliar with sobriety. But when God saved my soul, he took that addiction away and crucified it with Jesus on the cross. In fact, I changed so much after becoming a Christian that it started to freak out some of my family members—especially my cousin Lil Ron.

Lil Ron and I were really close growing up. We were more like brothers than cousins. I was always a small guy, so I needed a lionhearted cousin who was big in stature to watch my back in the concrete jungles we roamed daily. I mean, he literally saved my life a couple times. There is a lifetime of stories about Lil Ron and me, but I'll save that for another book. Our relationship was always clear. We rarely had to use words; we just knew what to expect from each other. But when I gave my life to Christ, our relationship became muddy. I don't think Lil Ron knew where I stood with him anymore.

He would ask me questions like "So, P, now that you a

WHEN YOU SHARE THE TRUTH WITH STRANGERS, IT'S SOMETIMES EASIER TO BE BOLD BECAUSE YOU CAN HIDE IN PLAIN SIGHT. BUT THERE'S NO AVOIDING FAMILY AND FRIENDS.

Christian, if a bunch of dudes were to show up right now and start something, would you ride for me?"

I told him, "Listen, cuzzo, if you were getting beat up, you know I would help protect you. But I ain't gonna go out there and ride with you no more or fight people like I used to."

And, man, that did not sit well with him. "You serious? Cuz, we your family! God ain't gonna be upset with you if you just defending your family."

At the time, I was torn. I didn't know how to explain to Lil Ron that I wasn't acting different, but my nature was new. I couldn't find the words to explain how much my heart was made aware that a holy God was watching me. How much doing the things I used to do would be me returning to the grave after Jesus did to my soul what he did to Lazarus's body. How he told death to let me go and called me to rise up from it. All I could think to say was "Cuz, I hear you. I just don't pursue a lifestyle that dishonors God anymore." I could feel Lil Ron's distaste. He felt like I was judging him and the family. He didn't understand that the God who had been my judge my whole life now called me friend. I tried to explain that I wasn't turning my back on Lil Ron. I was turning my back on the sin that kept me separate from God for so long. Lil Ron felt like I was choosing the family of God over my blood family. Yeah, our family was born with the same blood, but this new family I had in Christ was bought with blood far more valuable.

After I saw how Lil Ron reacted, I kind of avoided talking about my faith with my family and close friends because I was afraid it might make them feel uncomfortable, and a big part of me was afraid of being rejected. Here I was, bold lion in the faith with strangers, but around my family, I shrank and became a passive gnat, not wanting to be seen.

I was unsure how to reach those closest to me, but I soon found out there was good news. Unlike with strangers, when trying to reach the people you're closest to, time isn't as much of an enemy—time works for you if you use it wisely. And after a while, I realized that it wasn't so much a question of me approaching them as it was living my life in such a way that drew them to me.

WHEN TRYING TO REACH THE PEOPLE YOU'RE CLOSEST TO, TIME ISN'T AS MUCH OF AN ENEMY—TIME WORKS FOR YOU IF YOU USE IT WISELY.

Kinda like my grandmother.

My grandmother was an amazing Christian, a beautiful light for our family. She was the type of light that was set up on a hill and couldn't be hidden. She was generous, kind, loving, and always praying over us, and her life was always pointing us to Jesus. But growing up, my cousins and I were much more allured by the fast life of the streets than peeking into my grandmother's prayer closet. I was a kid growing up in the hood. I wanted to be cool. I wanted women to love me while not committing to any. I wanted to be like my uncle Stan.

Uncle Stan was the man in the city. He worked in the entertainment industry, and the dude knew just about everybody. He hung out with guys like Shaquille O'Neal, Ice Cube, Jermaine Dupri, and a bunch of other athletes and rappers, not just in Chicago, but also in Los Angeles, New York, Atlanta—all over the place. He was incredibly influential in my life.

When I was thirteen, on one tragic night on the south side, a bullet missed a crowd of folk and landed in my uncle's skull. I remember his funeral like it was this morning. That day was dark, and he was a still night star in a casket. My uncle was only thirty-one years young, and his life was gone because of some reckless man and his bullet.

Over the next several days, our entire family descended on my grandmother's house to grieve and to support one another. I, for one, couldn't wait to spend time with my other uncles. They were all brave men who knew grief by name. They had always given me confidence and made me feel stronger than I was. This time, though, it was different. Uncle Stan's death stripped all the brave from their chests. They sat around all day still as fragile stone, trying not to crumble, pretending not to be broken, trying to hide the river rising in their eyes every time they thought about their brother being gone. There is no scene sadder than hurting men afraid to be hurting men in public. Five days straight, everyone just walked around in shock, crying, and my grandmother was really struggling. Then one morning, she said to my mom, "I need to go into my room, lock the door, and get before the Lord."

My mom was like "Okay. I'll bring you a plate of something a little later and sit with you for a bit."

But my grandmother just shook her head. "No. I don't want

anything to eat, I don't want anything to drink, and I don't want any company. I just want to be by myself for one whole day—just me and the Lord."

Naturally, my mom was worried. My grandmother was closing in on seventy, and she'd just lost her youngest son. It was hard watching my mother trying to juggle both her and my grandmother's grief. So she tried again. "Mom, I really think I ought to be with you."

But my grandmother said, "Pam, no. Just leave me alone. I want to be by myself right now. I need to get before the Lord."

And with that, she walked into her bedroom, closed the door, and stayed there for twenty-four hours. And then the strangest thing happened. The next morning, it's hard to explain with words, but she just looked different. She came out of her room like a new song, smiling and going around the house comforting and praying for everyone. Her pain was still present near her smile, but she had a joy about her, and it single-handedly changed the atmosphere of the entire house. Man, I'd never seen anything like it. I didn't get it . . . but I'll tell you this: whatever it was she found in that room, it filled me with wonder.

From that day on, anytime something bad happened or something was bothering me, I looked to my grandmother. With all due respect for my uncles, I realized *she* was the backbone of our family. She never pushed her faith on me, told me I needed to repent, or asked me where I stood with God. She would just pray for me and encourage me and talk about her own relationship with God. I didn't fully understand where she was coming from, but I liked the way I felt when I was around her. I felt hopeful. I felt whole.

Years later, after I had met the Lord for myself, I sat down with my grandmother and said, "Grandma, when Uncle Stan died, it was really hard."

"Yes, it was," she said. "It was really hard."

"Can I ask you a question?" When she said I could, I said, "Four or five days after Uncle Stan died, you went into your room for a long time, and when you came out, you seemed . . . different. Even at the funeral, you seemed stronger than the rest of us. What happened to you in there?"

She paused, her light brown eyes glazing over as if she were staring back to that day. "Preston," she said, "when Stan was murdered, I felt like I was going to die. My pain felt unbearable. I could hardly bear the weight of walking around. I didn't even have the strength to be strong for my family, and I had never felt like that before. So I went into my room, and I said to the Lord, 'Lord, either give me the strength to be strong for my family or take me to glory.' And then I prayed. And I prayed. And I prayed. And, Preston, I began to feel the presence of God in a way I've never felt it before. The Lord visited me in my room that day, and his presence was so sweet that—at that moment—I entered into God's rest, and I've been there ever since."

Man, goose bumps began to swell on my skin. Then she said, "What we have to understand, Preston, is that Christians don't suffer the way the rest of the world suffers. Before I went into my room, I was suffering like my sons and my daughter who did not know the Lord. But once I found his presence, I had hope. That's what the Lord does, Preston. He gives us hope."

I get it now. Sharing our faith with our families or close friends doesn't look like it does with strangers out on the streets, where you're often asking questions, debating, and quoting Scripture. It looks more like my grandmother. It's living your faith consistently in a way that makes other people seek you out because you have something that they don't.

When my uncle died, my grandmother was sad and broken like we all were, but she wasn't sad and broken in the exact same way. She had hope because she knew a God who can't fail. She had peace because she served a God who told a storm to stop and the wind

SHARING YOUR FAITH WITH THOSE CLOSEST TO YOU IS LIVING CONSISTENTLY IN A WAY THAT MAKES OTHER PEOPLE SEEK YOU OUT BECAUSE YOU HAVE SOMETHING THAT THEY DON'T.

and waves obeyed like well-behaved children. The same God who sawed a sea in half to lead Israel into a land where slavery knew not their names and freedom sung them into a clear sky lived inside of her. Because of that she had a hope we didn't have. She had a God to run to who knew exactly how to tend to her grief. That's what drew me to her when I was hurting. It's what drew all of us to her—even if we didn't fully understand why.

That's what drew people to Jesus too. He had something in him that just made everything around him better—that could make people whole. That's why the bleeding woman became a blade and sliced her way through the crowd to touch the hem of Jesus' garment. That's why the friends of a man who was crippled tore a hole in a roof just to get him before Jesus. That's why wherever Jesus went, people brought people who were sick, disabled, deaf, blind, and demon possessed. They were all broken. They all wanted healing. And they knew where they could get it.

When I asked my grandmother what happened to her in her room that day, she literally did what 1 Peter 3:15 says. It might not seem like it, but at that moment, she was an apologist. She didn't chase me down or force her beliefs on me. She didn't try to tear down what I believed or make a big argument from Scripture. But she gave me a reason for the hope that was in her. She was able to do so because she lived her faith out loud before me. She loved me well and made herself available for me when I needed her. And she was ready when I asked my question. She made space for God to do a work in me. And isn't that what evangelism is? Letting God use your life to impact someone else's?

If you make yourself available to your friends and family members, when things get hard, they won't see you as a Christian looking to cast the first stone, but they'll see you as a rock they can stand on. Even if, like Lil Ron, they don't fully understand the change they see in you or the way you're living your life, they'll invariably be drawn to your stability, your optimism, and your confidence in the Lord.

Sometimes God may even allow somebody to go through a difficult season just so they will come to you. That has happened a lot in my life. My cousins may still call the streets home and live a life of sin, but when they are curious about God, are going through relationship problems, or get shot, they call me. When they get arrested, they call me. When they get scared or don't know what to do, they call me. When they're looking for hope, they call me.

The thing is, though, if all I ever did was force-feed them a God they don't have a taste for yet, they *wouldn't* call me. So I don't beat them over the head with Scripture, or get into heated debates with them, or lecture, or harass, or judge them. I just love them well. I make sure they know I'm still the same Preston who played ding-dong ditch and shared secrets about girls back in the day in Grandma's basement. I talk with them. And I pray with them. And when they ask me questions, I answer them with the same honesty old Preston had, but now I have God's truth and wisdom to give too.

I've flat out told my cousins, "Cuzzo, I don't think God desires this life for you. And I truly believe he's calling you to turn away from all this. He wants so much more for you. Cuz, it doesn't matter what you've done. God still loves you and wants you to come to him. But no matter what you decide, I want you to know that I love you and will always be here for you."

Again, that's the key distinction between street evangelism and sharing your faith with friends and family. More often than not, out on the street, it's one and done. You might only get to talk with someone for fifteen or twenty minutes before they have to move on, until your flight lands, or for the duration of an Uber ride. But with friends and family, you have history calling you back to each other. You can invest in these people over time because of what once was. You don't wake up one morning and say, "I think I'm going to try to lead so-and-so to Christ today." You just live and let God move. You let them see you live your faith out at home, at work, with your spouse, with your kids. Everywhere you go and in everything you do, you show them what it looks like to follow Jesus.

Or, to put it another way, you disciple them.

We've talked about evangelism (sharing your faith with others) and apologetics (defending your faith when others ask you questions about it). But why do any of these things if it's not to make disciples? The main goal is just what we looked at when we started, the great commission: "Jesus came and said to them, 'All authority in heaven and on earth has been given to me. Go therefore and make disciples of all nations, baptizing them in the name of the Father and of the Son and of the Holy Spirit, teaching them to observe all that I have commanded you. And behold, I am with you always, to the end of the age'" (Matthew 28:18-20).

The goal isn't to get someone to believe in Christianity and to walk away, content that we've smooth-talked their soul into heaven. It's to make disciples. The word *make* implies that it's a process—that it takes time.

Making disciples is a whole-life endeavor. And while we're not called to be involved at every step of the process, the great commission is for all of us. As I said before, not all of us are called to evangelize to strangers in the way that I do. Not everyone is called to teach. The Holy Spirit gives different gifts to different believers. But we are called to intentional living, to, as Paul says, "mak[e] the best use of the time" we have (Ephesians 5:16).

I know this can sound daunting and challenging to some, like I'm asking you to step outside yourself. But how else can we follow a God who stepped off an eternal throne to dwell in time to save us if we don't abandon our comfort to also pursue others? And much of the time, it looks like what my grandmother did for me: modeling what a Jesus-filled life looks like, being ready to answer other people's questions, and being a stable, God-honoring presence in your community so that others can know who to turn to when they have questions.

You saw this happen in my own story when I met Gary. But let me tell you about someone else who has shown me what it means to intentionally make disciples.

Before I became a Christian, Gary took me to a Puerto Rican neighborhood called Little Village to play a little midnight basketball. It was in this hot, musty little gym on the top floor of an old church, and it was run by this dude named Carlos, who was a street evangelist there. And I'm telling you, this was one rough hood—a ton of gangs and a lot of violence. That's why Carlos started opening the gym late at night. He was trying to provide a safe haven to keep kids off the streets.

Gary and I started to hoop with a bunch of Black and Puerto Rican kids, and in walked this white dude wearing a button-down shirt and khakis. He wasn't what I would call a big guy, but man, the dude looked fearless. He looked like he belonged.

I leaned over to Gary and whispered, "Who's the white dude?"

Gary laughed and said, "That's Brian Dye. Dude's a legend around here. We call him the Urban Missionary. Grew up right here in Little Village, then after college, he felt God calling him back to the hood to start a bunch of house churches."

I just looked at Gary like he was lying. I couldn't remember the last time I saw a white guy in this hood that wasn't wearing a badge.

"Yo, P, I'm telling you, when Brian first moved to his hood on the west side, there were murders on his block every week, but he dedicated his life to praying for these people, and, man, there has not been one murder since." As soon as Gary and Brian made eye contact, Brian broke into a giant smile and came right over. After they hugged it out, Gary took a step back and introduced us. "I was just filling Preston here in on a little of your origin story," he said, smiling.

"Yeah, man," I said. "Mad respect. It can't be easy being a white boy living in the hood." I regretted it almost the minute I said it, but Brian just nodded and smiled.

"Yeah . . . the week I moved in, some of the guys on the block shot into my house—completely shattered the bedroom window. One of the bullets just barely missed my wife." Then he laughed a little and said, "Apparently, they weren't too thrilled about a white guy moving in. They thought I was working for the police."

We talked a little more, and I left with the impression that he was a little crazy but cool.

Fast-forward a year and a half. I was working at RadioShack and doing spoken-word poetry shows in churches all across the city. A few of my videos had even gone viral on YouTube, so I was starting to make a bit of a name for myself. Anyway, after I finished up one event, I walked out to the lobby of the church, and Brian was standing there. Mind you, I had not seen this dude since that night in Little Village. He walked up to me, stuck his hand out, and reintroduced himself.

I shook his hand and said, "Yeah, man, I remember you. Good to see you again."

Then, out of nowhere, the dude said, "I just wanted to ask—do you have anybody walking with you?"

I was like "Walking with me? You mean like back home?" I mean, it was nice of him to offer, but of the two of us, I was a lot less likely to get hassled in this neck of the hood.

"No, man," he laughed, "I mean mentoring you—discipling you."

Instantly I got suspicious. I thought, *Man, this dude is trying to latch on to me because my poetry is starting to take off.* So I just said, "Yeah . . . thanks, man, but I'm cool. I got people in my life. I'm just doing my thing for the Lord, you feel me?"

Dude didn't give up, though. For some reason, he kept pursuing me. He would pop up at my shows and tell me stuff like "God is just laying you on my heart, man. You're starting to make quite an impact in the community, and I think you could use someone to guide you."

I finally just gave him my number, knowing full well I wasn't going to respond to any of his calls or texts. I was just trying to shake him.

Over the next couple of months, he would text me stuff like "God laid you on my heart again this morning. How are you doing?" But I never responded.

After a while, I started hearing from other people, "Brian said you aren't responding to any of his texts." I thought, *Man, what is up with this cat? He's got other people checking on me now?* So I called my then-friend, now-wife, Jackie, and said, "Yo, this white guy keeps following me around trying to disciple me. I don't trust the dude, you know what I'm saying? It's weird."

At first, she was like "Yeah, I wouldn't trust that either." But as the weeks passed and Brian kept reaching out, she started to change her tune.

"You know, Preston," she said, "maybe the Lord doesn't want you to dictate what discipleship looks like for you. This dude's been pretty persistent. Maybe you shouldn't reject his offer of mentorship and discipleship just because it's not coming in the package you want it to come in."

Dang. I couldn't deny that her words were wise and real. Thank God I married her later on.

So, I called Brian up and said, "Hey, what's up, man? Listen, I know I've been avoiding you. I'm just going to be honest with you. I don't trust you."

"Can I ask why?" he said.

"Well, for one thing, I've never had a white guy following me around at my shows. Actually, now that I think about it, you are the only white guy at my shows. And I don't really know your intentions."

He just laughed. "Well, it's good that you're honest. To me, that's one of the things that makes you special. And I'll gladly tell you my intentions. First off, I'm not trying to mooch off your platform or your popularity. I really don't care about that. I just think very highly of you, Preston. I think you have a great voice. I think that God has a great call on your life. And I think that you're on your way to becoming a great leader. But time and time again, I've seen leaders get taken under because they don't have people to speak truth to them and keep them on the right track. I'm going on forty, and I still have somebody who walks with me and disciples me. And I think that what God has taught me over the years will help me help you to be the best man of God and minister that you can be."

I suddenly felt guilty for how I'd curved Brian for so long. I'd never had anybody, let alone a pastor, speak to me like that before.

Long story short, I decided to give him a chance. And I'm telling you, this dude was the real deal. He told me, "I want you to come to my house. I want you to see how I live. I want you to see how I treat my wife. I want you to see how I work, how I interact with people at church and in the community."

He explained, "That's what life-on-life discipleship is, Preston. It's not just meeting at Starbucks once a week to go over a handful of Scriptures. It's literally doing life with people."

Really, what Brian was doing with me was exactly what Jesus did with the apostles. He invited them into his life so they could learn, firsthand, how to be more like him. When two of John's disciples saw Jesus walking by, they began to follow him. Jesus noticed and turned and asked, "What are you seeking?" (John 1:38). They responded by saying, "Where are you staying?" They were not asking where he was staying because they wanted to see what his house looked like. Instead, they were saying "Jesus, teach us by showing us how you live." Notice how they didn't say, "Jesus, when is the next time you're preaching in front of a crowd or teaching in the synagogue?" But isn't that the way many of us learn today? We follow our favorite teachers and preachers around the world to Christian events and conferences instead of looking for faithful men and women we can learn from up close. Don't get me wrong, there is nothing wrong with Christian events and conferences—I speak at them all the time—and Jesus spoke to large crowds. But that's not all he did. He mostly poured into twelve disciples who poured into others. We're not all called to be public teachers and preachers, but we are all called to keep the great commission in this way. This is how we make disciples of all nations. This is what Brian being in my life did for me.

Gary may have taught me what it meant to be a Christian, but Brian taught me what it meant to be a mature Christian. He taught me how to be a Christian husband, a Christian brother, and a Christian leader.

My evangelism flourished under his leadership as he recognized my gifts and helped me to cultivate them. I wouldn't have even known I was an evangelist if it hadn't been for Brian.

Brian single-handedly transformed the way I approach discipleship. But more than that, Brian single-handedly transformed my *life*. In fact, that's what evangelism looks like on a personal level: discipleship. It's not just throwing down Scriptures or, like Brian said, doing a once-a-week, hour-long Bible study at Starbucks. Those things aren't bad. But if we really want people to see the hope that is within us, there is no better way to do that than by spending time together and letting them see what that hope looks like in each facet of our lives.

God didn't create us to do life alone. He created us to live in community with one another. He wants us to challenge and strengthen one another, like how "iron sharpens iron" (Proverbs 27:17). Accepting Christ as your Lord and Savior is just step one. Learning how to live like Christ in ways that will naturally draw others to you like moths to a flame? That takes time. That takes discipleship. In my case, it took a white dude with a heart for helping young Christian men realize their full potential and a willingness to open up his home and his life and invest in one of them over the long haul.

But the thing about Brian is, it wasn't just me. For his fortieth birthday, Brian's wife, Heidi, threw a surprise party for him. A couple hundred people showed up. At one point, Heidi got up on stage and said, "If you have been discipled or mentored by Brian Dye at some point over the last fifteen years, please stand up," and seventy-five young men from the ages of thirteen to thirty-five rose to their feet.

Man, that's what sharing the hope that is within you is all about.

Not every one of us will be like Brian Dye, with seventy-five people we've actively discipled.

But the thing is, we all need people like him in our lives who can walk through life with us and help cultivate our gifts. In 2 Timothy, Paul writes to his mentee in the faith, Timothy, and says, "You, however, have followed my teaching, my conduct, my aim in life, my faith, my patience, my love, my steadfastness, my persecutions and sufferings that happened to me. . . . But as for you, continue in what you have learned and have firmly believed, knowing from whom you learned it" (2 Timothy 3:10-11, 14).

He then goes on to say, "I charge you in the presence of God and of Christ Jesus . . . : preach the word; be ready in season and out of season; reprove, rebuke, and exhort, with complete patience and teaching. . . . Always be sober-minded, endure suffering, do the work of an evangelist, fulfill your ministry" (2 Timothy 4:1-2, 5).

In other words, Paul tells Timothy, "Hey, man, you've seen me do life—and a lot of it's been hard. Well, now it's your turn. Get out there and teach others what you have learned from me—oh, and by the way, do it with gentleness and respect."

Hand on heart, I think that's a near-perfect picture of what evangelism ought to look like—constantly growing and helping others grow in faith, day in and day out.

That's what Gary did. He let me go everywhere with him. As he was doing life. As he went to the bank. As he was talking with someone. As he became convicted about his sin. That was what ultimately showed me the kind of relationship with Christ I wanted. Gary lived his Christian life out loud, and he let me be a part of it.

So did Brian. I had gifts in evangelism, but I became an even more effective apologist and evangelist once Brian came into my life and discipled me.

So, yeah . . . walking up to strangers on the street and entering into a conversation with them about their faith can be hard. That's one way to do evangelism, and that's where my gifts and calling lie.

Living your life in such a way that other people start walking up to you to find out what you have that they don't? That's a call for us all.

Welcoming them into your life, letting them get up close and personal so they can see and experience firsthand the hope that is within you, and then helping them do the same? Man, that's unapologetic apologetics. That's how to tell the truth in the best way imaginable.

Still think you can't do it? Keep chillin' with me.

7

DON'T GIVE UP

ONE OF THE CENTRAL MESSAGES of this book is that I think we overcomplicate evangelism. Sharing our faith isn't just about arguing with people of other faiths over discrepancies in doctrine or Scripture. Sometimes it is, and we should try to be ready. But at all times, it's about reflecting Christ's love to those closest to us, reaching out to people who are hurting, sharing our personal testimony, and intentionally living our lives as witnesses to who Jesus is.

My aim in this chapter is to encourage you in sharing your faith by showing you that evangelism doesn't have to look the same for everybody, that your fears are not the only part of the equation, and that God is ultimately in charge of the results of our evangelism.

Not everybody is called to share their faith in the way that I am. I mean, when I get in an Uber ride, I'm automatically looking around to see if my driver has anything hanging from his rearview mirror that might indicate he belongs to another religion so I can ask him about it. That's just my personality. I'm outgoing, and I like to start conversations with people.

But when my wife, Jackie, gets into an Uber, she'll put her earbuds in and go straight to sleep. She's more of an introvert, and that's okay—that's her personality. But make no mistake: she's also great at sharing her faith. She just does it differently. Jackie's thing might not be walking up to someone on the street and starting a conversation, but when she gets comfortable with someone, I'm telling you, God uses that woman in amazing ways. She challenges people in their faith. She builds people up, and she disciples young women and moms. She might not be comfortable in as many situations as I am, but she prays for God to use her. And God does use her—often. He just uses us differently because he created us different.

What I'm saying is that evangelism looks different for different people. And God uses people differently too.

I'll give you a prime example. A few years ago, we were flying from Virginia to Atlanta, and as we were walking through the airport, I saw some Jehovah's Witnesses passing out tracts. So, naturally, I was like "Babe, we have forty-five minutes until our flight leaves, and our gate is right there, so I'm going to talk to these guys."

And she was like "Okay. I'll go get us some food. Peace out."

Jackie went her way, and I went mine. After I finished talking to the Jehovah's Witnesses, I headed over to the restaurant area by our gate. I was surprised to see Jackie with her head bowed, praying with the waitress.

After they finished praying, I introduced myself to the waitress and asked if I was interrupting anything. Jackie said, "Nah, you're good. I just came over here to get some food for us, and when I ordered for two, she asked me who else I was getting food for. I told her it was for my husband. She asked me where you were, so I said, 'He's over there talking to some Jehovah's Witnesses.'"

It turned out the waitress was raised by Jehovah's Witnesses, and her family really messed with her head and drove her away from faith, so Jackie started talking with her, and the next thing you know, she was praying with her. Later Jackie told me, "I just felt like God was telling me to share the gospel with her, so I did."

My point is, Jackie might not be as comfortable around strangers as I am or actively seek to engage people the way that I do, but she does ask God to provide opportunities for her to speak on his behalf, and when those opportunities come her way, she's ready. She doesn't shy away from them. And you know what? That readiness? That openness to doing God's will? That willingness to step out of her comfort zone and speak truth and life into a fellow image bearer? That, more than anything, is what it takes to be successful in sharing our faith.

Now, I know what you're thinking. *Yo, Preston, that's easy for you to say. You basically talk to people for a living and, man, you live and breathe for these conversations. That's not me.* I hear you.

But believe me, as extroverted as I am, there have been plenty of times when I've been on my way home from a conference after talking with people for two days straight, and I just collapsed into the back of the Uber. Sometimes, the conversation has looked like this:

"So, where you coming from?"

"I was working."

"So, what do you do?"

"I'm a speaker."

"What kind of stuff do you talk about?"

I mean, the driver will literally throw the door wide open for me to share my faith, and sometimes I just don't feel like walking through it. Or I'll be at a party or out to dinner with a group of people, and I'll see an opening but think, *Man, I'm at a party . . . do I really want to get into this right now?*

THE GREAT COMMISSION WASN'T JUST FOR THE APOSTLES; IT'S FOR ALL OF US.

But as tempted as I may be to just let the moment pass, I try not to let it because this is what God has called me to do.

All believers have a responsibility to share their faith. The great commission wasn't just for the apostles; it's for all of us. We are called to be salt and light to the world, in both word and deed. I mean, look around. We live in a world filled with people who don't know God. Even if we don't always feel like sharing our faith, this isn't an excuse for disobedience. Because in many respects, sharing our faith *is* an act of obedience. It's about intentionally engaging with the world around us.

One time me and my friends LB and Nico were at a restaurant, and the waitress who was serving us just looked exhausted. So after she brought us our food, LB acknowledged that. He said, "You seem really tired."

"Yeah . . . I'm going through a lot right now," she told us.

So Nico said, "Can I ask what you're going through?"

"I've just got a lot going on with my son," she said.

"Is he sick?" I asked.

And then it all just spilled right out of her. "No. About a week and a half ago, he brought a gun to school. He got it from a friend of his, and it turns out it was loaded, so they arrested him, and now he's in a juvenile detention center." At this point, her eyes started to well over.

"How old is he?" asked LB.

"He's fourteen. He's not a bad kid. This is the first real trouble he's ever gotten into. I've been working overtime trying to pay for his lawyers. I just don't know what to do."

Man, you could tell she was beside herself. I told her that I used to be in trouble with the law a lot when I was his age and assured her that everything would be okay. Then I asked, "Would it be okay if we prayed for you?"

She said yes, so we prayed for her right there at the table, and when we were done, she asked us, "Are y'all Christians?" We said yes, and then one by one, we each shared our testimonies with her. We only talked with her for about ten minutes, but I think it did her heart a world of good not only to unburden herself but to hear about how three dudes from the hood—none of us having a pretty past with the law—turned themselves around after accepting Christ as their Lord and Savior.

Before we left, she asked us where we went to church. We told her, and I got the impression that as soon as her son got out of juvie, she was going to take him there.

Now, we didn't go to that restaurant with the goal of sharing our faith. We were just chillin' and the opportunity presented itself. But it happened because we were being intentional about our faith and our call to love one another. We saw that our waitress was struggling, and instead of treating her pain as invisible, we helped her carry her problems. Chivalry shouldn't be dead when men who serve the God who defeated death are around. Isn't empathy that Christlike trait inside us that makes us adopt someone's struggles as our own?

That's what the great commission is all about. When Jesus instructed his followers to "go and make disciples of all nations" (Matthew 28:19), he wasn't telling them to go to a specific place. He just said, "Go"—as in, "as you go about your daily life and encounter people who are lost and hurting and need to hear my message of salvation, give it to them."

We were created to live in community with one another, and Jesus commanded us to always be on the lookout for opportunities to share our faith. Paul calls us "ambassadors for Christ" (2 Corinthians 5:20), and fulfilling that call should take us out of our churches and into our workplaces, our communities, and everywhere we go.

If you're driving in a carpool while listening to Christian

music and your passenger asks you, "Why are you listening to that?"—that's an opportunity to share your faith.

If a friend or coworker starts telling you about a difficult season they're going through—that's an opportunity to share your faith.

If you're wearing a cross around your neck and someone admires it—that's an opportunity to talk about your faith. That's why I created Bold Apparel. I wanted to create organic opportunities for people to start conversations about their faith. When people see a hoodie or a T-shirt with "Jesus & Therapy" written on it, they get curious. And if the Holy Spirit is working on them, they might just ask, "What's your shirt mean?"

God provides us with opportunities to share or talk about our faith with others all the time. What we do with them is up to us.

Paul told the Galatian church, "Let us not grow weary of doing good, for in due season we will reap, if we do not give up" (Galatians 6:9). And that's my goal: to encourage you to not give up. Because telling others the truth of the gospel *is* "doing good," and I believe that we, too, "will reap, if we do not give up"—even if the reaping is not always what we expect.

I think a lot of times, we opt out of sharing our faith because we're afraid that we're going to offend someone or that we're going to make a mistake and say the wrong thing. And you know what? We *are* going to offend someone—Jesus tells us as much. He said, "If the world hates you, know that it has hated me before it hated you. If you were of the world, the world would love you as its own; but because you are not of the world, but I chose you out of the world, therefore the world hates you" (John 15:18-19). But he also tells us, "Blessed are you when others revile you and persecute you and utter all kinds of evil against you falsely on my account. Rejoice and be glad, for your reward is great in heaven" (Matthew 5:11-12).

And yes, we might say or do the wrong thing. We are imperfect humans. But remember, the Holy Spirit—not our words—convicts the heart. That isn't to say that we shouldn't be careful about what we say, or that we can be ignorant or insensitive or throw caution to the wind and say whatever we want. God still wants us to demonstrate good character, to respect and honor others, and to present his message clearly. But even if we do say the wrong thing, God can still use it.

I mean, look at how badly I jacked up my first few interactions with John. And yet God still used those conversations to help me learn the correct way to defend my faith. And who's to say that something I said to John—even in those early heated conversations—didn't give him a check in his spirit or challenge him to think about some of his beliefs a little differently?

Like any good father, God wants us to be successful. And if we ask him for his help, he will give it to us. I can attest to that personally. I can't tell you how many times I've been in the middle of a debate, got hit with a question that I couldn't answer, asked God for help, and all of a sudden, had a response

WHILE WE ARE GOING
TO MAKE MISTAKES,
THE GOOD NEWS
IS THAT WE SERVE
A SOVEREIGN GOD
WHO EXCELS AT
USING IMPERFECT
PEOPLE TO DO
HIS WILL.

just pop into my head. God is faithful, and when we demonstrate our dependence on him, he honors that. And when you realize that God is with you—man, there's nothing you can't do.

John 15:5 says, "I am the vine; you are the branches. Whoever abides in me and I in him, he it is that bears much fruit, for apart from me you can do nothing." I truly believe that. The more I stay in close proximity to the Lord and remain connected to him, the more I'm ready to minister to people when the opportunity arises. But when there's a disconnect between me and the Lord, nine times out of ten, there's going to be a disconnect between me and the people I'm talking to. That's just how it goes. So stay close to the Lord, both by studying his Word and in prayer.

While we are going to make mistakes, the good news is that we serve a sovereign God who excels at using imperfect people to do his will. The Bible is full of examples of God using imperfect messengers to communicate his message. Moses wasn't good at speaking. Jeremiah was too young. Jonah tried to run away. Jesus' disciples were fishermen and tradesmen, not the religious elite. Peter straight-up denied Christ three times, but God still used him to help build his church. When Paul was in prison, he wrote about others who were preaching "out of selfish ambition." And his response? "What then? Only that in every way, whether in pretense or in truth, Christ is proclaimed, and in that I rejoice" (Philippians 1:17-18). If God can use even the willfully disobedient, he can use our best efforts.

God can use anything. I don't think our minds can even comprehend all the work that God is doing behind the scenes.

He's not asking us to be perfect. He's simply asking us to be faithful. He'll take care of the rest.

⊰⊱⊰⊱⊰

Another reason some of us shrink from sharing our faith is the fear of failure. We think that if we don't bring people to a point of conversion, we have failed. Let me correct that faulty thinking right now. It is not our job to convert people.

The author of Hebrews calls Jesus "the founder and perfecter [the *finisher*] of our faith" (Hebrews 12:2). We're not doing the final work. We're not even doing the *initial* work. The triune God calls people to himself, and God is the finisher that comes in after us, seeing things through to completion and making them right—kind of like an assembly line. Nothing is finished until it goes through the whole system. You and me? We're just one step in the process, but God is in control of the process.

God's pursuit of our souls is often a slow cook and not the result of a defining act or person. He will use people to get our hearts tender and ready to receive him. Five years from now, you might be part of a person's testimony. They might say, "Man, it all started when this woman shared the gospel with me at a party" or "I was listening to two dudes debating a passage of Scripture over lunch one day, and it made me think." You and I? We are not God. We're just his ambassadors, sharing his Good News and hopefully setting people on the path that will eventually lead them to him.

This should be an encouragement for us. We put too much

pressure on ourselves while sharing the gospel with people. I think the church has conditioned us to expect right-now results. We've grown accustomed to call-and-response culture, the altar calls followed by counting the souls that say yes to Jesus each Sunday. This isn't always a bad thing. I think in many ways our expectation of immediate change bears witness to the faith we have been given, that "if anyone is in Christ, he is a new creation. The old has passed away; behold, the new has come" (2 Corinthians 5:17). The change from who we were to who we are is so drastic, we think it must have been sudden. When the gospel goes forth, we expect God to move *now*.

But when we "go and make disciples of all nations," we can set ourselves up for failure if we don't understand that God moves in more ways than what we're used to seeing.

This is why some of us may shy away from evangelism. We don't want people to reject our efforts. We don't want to feel like failures. But what is failure when we're working for the God who created the universe? People don't reject *us*; they reject the God we serve.

IF WE LOOK AT OUR OWN STORIES OF HOW WE CAME TO BELIEVE IN CHRIST, WE'LL SEE THAT IT WAS USUALLY MORE OF A SLOW COOK THAN WE THOUGHT.

But more than that, what looks like failure isn't always. And even more than that, if we look at our own stories of how we came to believe in Christ, we'll see that it was usually more of a slow cook than we thought. Remember the first time I heard the gospel at my girlfriend's house church? The pastor that gave the gospel that Sunday would later hear about fights I would get into in the neighborhood and tell me, "You heard me preach many Sundays about how Christ died for you, but you still won't choose him! You still insist on living a lifestyle that will bring you destruction!" What he didn't know is that God used him to change my life the first time I heard him. I didn't stop sinning against God, but I did become aware of my sins in a way that left me without an excuse. That day, God used that pastor to plant a seed in my life that others, later on, would water. God was drawing me to himself for years. He used a local neighborhood pastor to convict me of sin, he used my friend Chris's death to wake me up that I needed to change, and he used my grandmother's and Aunt Denise's influence, as well as Gary's life and witness, to show me that Jesus was the answer I was looking for. But it was the combination—how God used all of them together—that caused me to surrender my life to him. It took time.

The Corinthian church had a similar problem of not seeing how God had been moving among them. They were getting caught up in honoring one leader over another, so Paul set them straight. He wrote, "What then is Apollos?" (Apollos was one of the other leaders.) "What is Paul? Servants through whom you believed, as the Lord assigned to each. I planted, Apollos watered, but God gave the growth" (1 Corinthians 3:5-6).

Don't be discouraged if you don't see the growth. God works in his own good timing, and we won't always see the fruit of our labor. He just calls us to be faithful to perform our part.

That said, we need to be prepared, too, that some people may never come to Christ.

There are two kinds of people you will invariably encounter when you share your faith—those who don't know God whose hearts are open, and those who don't know God whose hearts are closed. How can you tell the difference? Let's go back to the story of the man born blind in John 9 (which we looked at in chapter 5).

If you'll recall, Jesus healed the man who was born blind twice—first restoring his physical sight and then restoring his spiritual sight. Now, after Jesus restored the man's sight, those who knew the man who had been born blind asked him who healed him. He replied, "The man called Jesus made mud and anointed my eyes and said to me, 'Go to Siloam and wash.' So I went and washed and received my sight" (John 9:11).

These people brought him before the Pharisees, who also asked him who restored his sight. The blind man told them it was Jesus, "a prophet" (John 9:17). The Pharisees were still skeptical and unwilling to believe that Jesus could have healed the man, so they questioned the man's parents—just to confirm that he had actually been born blind. Mind you, this dude had been sitting outside in public begging for years, so the fact that the Pharisees still felt the need to confirm the guy's story shows just how hard their hearts were towards Jesus.

After his parents confirmed that yes, their son had, in fact, been born blind, the Pharisees summoned the man again and said, "Give glory to God. . . . What did he do to you? How did he open your eyes?"

The man replied, "I have told you already, and you would not listen. Why do you want to hear it again?" (John 9:24, 26-27).

I mean, dude's got a point. How many times do they need to hear the truth before they choose to believe it? But the Pharisees were unwilling to believe that Jesus was the Messiah. And why? Because he miraculously healed the man of a debilitating lifetime affliction on the Sabbath, and only a sinner would dare to change someone's life on the Sabbath.

Man, I need a minute.

⤙⤙⤙⤙

Okay . . .

So then the man who had been born blind calls the Pharisees out, essentially saying, "Listen: y'all believe whatever you want, but I couldn't see, and now I can, and the only way that could have happened is if Jesus is from God, because God doesn't listen to sinners, and without God's help, he couldn't have healed me" (see John 9:31-33).

And how did the Pharisees respond to that? They kicked the poor dude out of the synagogue.

That's when Jesus arrives on the scene. By the way, I love this part of the story. I love that Jesus comes back for the rejected. This man had been begging outside the synagogue most of his life, on the outskirts of society, but he was not fully rejected until he testified that Jesus was the one who healed him. And that was when Jesus came back. Jesus comes back for hurting, neglected, wounded people.

"Do you believe in the Son of Man?" Jesus asks the man.

Now, remember, the man had never actually seen Jesus before, so he asks, "Who is he, sir, that I may believe in him?" (John 9:35-36).

And as soon as Jesus tells him, "That would be me," the man instantly falls at Jesus' feet and worships him. By physically restoring his sight, Jesus opened the man's eyes spiritually to be receptive to the fact that he is the Messiah. His heart was softened. He was ready.

But the Pharisees' hearts were so hardened by pride and obsession with the law that even though they had witnessed a miracle in plain sight, they remained spiritually blind.

That's why Jesus says, "For judgment I came into this world, that those who do not see may see, and those who see may become blind" (John 9:39). I mean, that's a pretty powerful statement.

Then he says to the Pharisees, "If you were blind, you would have no guilt; but now that you say, 'We see,' your guilt remains" (John 9:41). Jesus essentially tells them, "If your disbelief were a result of sheer ignorance, I might be able to let that slide. But because you claim to know God but still choose not to see him, there's nothing more I can do."

I think in evangelism, we have to understand the difference between receptive and unreceptive hearts. If we don't, we'll find ourselves pouring time and energy into people whose hearts are closed to the truth at the expense of those whose hearts are open.

The question is, How can we tell?

I believe, in some ways, we can tell a person's heart is receptive by talking with them and by really listening to what they say. Take, for example, an agnostic couple I talked to about Jesus for my YouTube channel, who told me they were neglected and misused by the church. I could hear that they were hurting, yet they were open. But there was also a guy who was standing just off camera threatening to beat me up. I remember thinking, *Man, God really wants to reach this couple. I can almost feel God's heart for them.* But I could also feel the enemy using this other dude to antagonize and distract me—picking at everything I was saying, trying to veer me off course and give my attention to him because he was upset by the work I was doing, in the same way the Pharisees were mad at the work Jesus was doing. In that moment, I could see receptive hearts and unreceptive hearts up close.

But that's not to say we should ignore the people whose hearts have been hardened against God. Jesus still engaged with the Pharisees—he even got through to some of them. And Christian history is full of unexpected converts—starting with the apostle Paul himself, who persecuted the church but came to believe when Jesus appeared to him on the way to Damascus. While we might be able to gauge current receptivity, there's no way for us to know exactly who God will reach or how he will reach them.

The main thing to remember is that whether people ultimately choose to surrender their lives to Jesus is not up to you or me. Our job is simply to be faithful and entrust the results to God.

Jesus calls his followers to be obedient. To step outside our comfort zones and offer his life-giving message to lost and hurting people. He calls us to serve them, and he calls us to love them.

It can be discouraging sometimes when it feels like our message falls on unreceptive hearts, but that's why we need Paul's encouragement to "not grow weary of doing good" (Galatians 6:9). We can't tell today how God will ultimately use our witness. Paul writes to the church in Corinth, "Be steadfast, immovable, always abounding in the work of the Lord, knowing that in the Lord your labor is not in vain" (1 Corinthians 15:58). Because Jesus is responsible for the process, start to finish, our work for him is never wasted, is never a failure.

So don't give up. Using the gifts and personality God has given you, through your fears and discouragement, be bold in how you tell the truth to others.

8

BE BOLD

I LOVE THE WORD BOLD. As I said, I even named my clothing line Bold Apparel.

A lot of people think boldness means simply fearlessness, but I think there's more to it than that. Before we talk about what boldness is, though, let's explore what prevents us from being bold in the first place: fear.

We talked a little about fear in the last chapter. Fear can be such a crippling thing in evangelism. Fear makes our tongues forget language when God tells us to speak. We fear how other created humans will cut us with their stare if we tell them about their pitch-black sin and their great need for the Son.

But why do we often have fear in our possession when the

God who created us didn't give us that spirit (see 2 Timothy 1:7)? Could it be that we fear people more than we fear the God who created them? Maybe we fear not being accepted by those closest to us when we share our faith, like the fear I had with my cousins when I first became a Christian. Maybe we fear the loss of money or fame or followers if we repeat the words of Jesus and dare to look like him in public. Maybe we fear cancel culture after seeing how people tried to erase a few Christians we know for talking too holy on the Internet. The reason for this fear can often be found in a word that can be synonymous with fearfulness: cowardice.

I know the word *coward* can fall on the ear harshly. But if we're honest, a lot of us have had cowardly moments during our walks with Jesus. Yeah, even me, the guy who started a clothing brand called Bold Apparel. The definition of a coward is one who lacks courage to endure dangerous or unpleasant things—things like a cross and the weight of carrying one. But I want you to do me a favor. I want you to think about all the times you were a coward. Think about all the times you became mute, afraid to speak up because of what it might cost you. Have those moments arrived in your memory? Cool. Now do me another favor. If you thought about those times and shame grabbed you against your will, I want you to tell it to let you go! Why? Because shame has no place in a saint who still has a chance to be used by God.

Think about Peter and how that rooster told him he was a coward three times when he denied Jesus after he was arrested. But aren't we still the church God built on a rock called Peter?

Didn't God still use Peter greatly? God's grace was sufficient enough to give Peter a second chance to get it right, and his same grace is sufficient for us too. You are not a coward if only you would believe you are who God says you are. Let it go.

Now that we've let our shame loose on the wind and remembered grace, I would be remiss—unloving, even—if I didn't warn you of something. Even though every sunrise is another chance to give your cowardice to God, please make sure you don't die a coward. The Bible says that cowards will not inherit the Kingdom of God (see Revelation 21:8). What's even more alarming is that Scripture lumps cowards in with unbelievers, the corrupt, the immoral, murderers, those who practice witchcraft, and more. Why is being a coward so serious to God? Most of us don't respect a coward. But the eternal God of heaven says a coward will not even live with him forever.

I believe this has just as much to do with who a coward is as the holiness of God. This is what I mean: when being a coward is who someone is, it is impossible for them to follow God. They will always look to other things before they turn to God for help.

For a better understanding of what I mean, let's compare Peter to Judas. Peter and Judas both denied Jesus. They both acted cowardly and felt guilty afterwards. Peter's guilt led him to godly sorrow and repentance. But not Judas. Judas took a noose and hung his guilt. Instead of turning to the God who was about to die on a tree for all sin, he put absent hope in suicide and hung himself on another tree. The coward will always look for a way out instead of looking to the God who died to bring them into the Kingdom. So the coward will not inherit the Kingdom of God like the others listed in Revelation 21:8, essentially for the same reason. They're not looking for the Kingdom. They are always looking for a way out.

Maybe fear of people isn't your thing. Maybe you're reading this and saying to yourself, *This ain't none of me. I only fear the Father, the Son he sent, and the Holy Spirit that leads me to all truth.* But the way I see it, boldness isn't about doing what you are afraid to do. It's about doing what God is telling you to do. Boldness is more about obedience to God than being fearless before people. If we are convinced that God is someone worth following and obeying, please believe he can give you the boldness to say yes to him, even when it might cost you something. To paint a picture for us, I want our minds to travel to a man in the Bible that most people don't talk about often. A man named Joseph of Arimathea.

Yeah . . . that guy—a Pharisee. After the last chapter, probably not who you were expecting, right? Hear me out.

Joseph of Arimathea is only mentioned once in the Gospels, which is probably why you don't think about him very much. However, Matthew, Mark, Luke, and John all give an account of Joseph's story, which, personally, I think is a sign of mad respect.

What I especially like about reading their accounts is that they all give different details. Matthew tells us that Joseph was rich (see Matthew 27:57). Mark tells us that he was a prominent member of the Sanhedrin (see Mark 15:43). Luke tells us that he was "a good and righteous man, who had not consented to

BOLDNESS IS
MORE ABOUT
OBEDIENCE
TO GOD THAN
BEING FEARLESS
BEFORE PEOPLE.

[the Sanhedrin's] decision and action" and that "he was looking for the kingdom of God" (Luke 23:50-51). And finally, John tells us that Joseph stayed quiet about his allegiance to Jesus because he feared retribution by the Sanhedrin.

We don't know exactly when Joseph's heart first said yes to God. The Bible doesn't tell us how God was able to get Joseph's hallelujah, since he was coming from the same group of men who hated Jesus, or what the tipping point was. But we do know that after the Crucifixion, Joseph went to Pilate and asked his permission to bury Jesus' body, and this act of boldness thundered across history.

You see, the most dangerous time to follow Jesus was not when he was alive; it was after he had been crucified, after he was considered a curse and a criminal, a blasphemer and a false prophet. The Crucifixion snatched the life from his bones. But the religious leaders who put Jesus on trial snatched away his innocence. The point is, when Jesus gave up the ghost on that shameful cross and the sky turned black, it became scary hours for those who followed him—which is why the disciples went into hiding after the Crucifixion.

Think about that for a second.

After Jesus was killed, all of the disciples—his homies, his inner circle, who had followed him in public for three years—all ran away and hid. With the exception of John, they didn't even show up for the Crucifixion. And a secret disciple named Joseph of Arimathea, who had been hiding until this time, popped up his head.

Once I heard a preacher shout in a sermon, "Joseph of

Arimathea was a coward! Dude believed in Jesus but never said anything because he was afraid!" But was he? And even if he was at first, man, did buddy make up for it. I mean, when he went to Pilate to ask for Jesus' body, he didn't know how Pilate would react. He didn't know if Pilate would say, "Oh, you want to honor the rebel we just killed? Let's find a cross for you too." The man literally risked his life to make sure that Jesus had a proper Jewish burial.

When the Romans executed people on crosses, they were usually left to rot on them as a warning to other would-be rebels. Their bodies were just left to bake under a Middle Eastern sun. And had it not been for Joseph of Arimathea, that might have been Jesus' fate.[3] But Joseph knew in his heart that Jesus was who he said he was, so he didn't even flinch to ask for the body of Jesus. He couldn't. Jesus' body had to be buried that day, before the Sabbath began. Fortunately, Jesus had already been fully anointed in oil two days earlier by Mary in Bethany. Still . . . given the time constraints, someone had to act, and quickly. Joseph did.

Yes, it's true that during Jesus' life, Joseph's discipleship to Jesus was hushed and buried deep beneath his breath. But God gave him the boldness to stand up for his faith when it could cost him the most. As a member of the Sanhedrin, he risked his fortune. He risked his social standing. He risked his position. He risked his reputation. And of course, he risked his very life. He risked *everything*.

Joseph's story should be an encouragement to those who think they're just not "bold." His story shows us that boldness is not a personality trait. Rather, it is the willingness to act when God is calling you to. When God gets our yes, the world will experience our boldness. It can be easy for all of us to judge Joseph for his earlier silence. But ask yourself this question: *Will my love for Jesus still be as loud when I'm surrounded by people who hate him?* When everybody

BOLDNESS IS NOT A PERSONALITY TRAIT. RATHER, IT IS THE WILLING-NESS TO ACT WHEN GOD IS CALLING YOU TO.

around you loves and worships Jesus, boldness is not required as much. But what would you do if God called you to stand before someone like Pilate to speak or act on God's behalf?

Believe it or not, in many ways, he already has. At the core, this is what evangelism is. It is being willing to put your social status on the line, your career on the line, your friendships on the line, and even your life on the line to proclaim the name of Jesus to a world that hates him. If we are going to fulfill the great commission and make disciples of all nations, at some point Jesus is calling us all to walk in some measure of boldness. The Bible says that Jesus' body was beaten beyond recognition. Can you imagine being Joseph for a moment? Imagine how he must've felt, being a part of a group of men who dressed them-selves in hate for Jesus. How helpless he felt watching Jesus' mother, Mary, look on with eyes like two sunless mornings as her innocent son was tortured. And after Jesus had died, feeling compelled to care for his battered body. He didn't come to fight with the other members of the council or Pilate. He just wanted to finally honor the King he loved in secret, out loud.

I believe there is a coming time when our evangelism will call us to this type of boldness. Children of God, we still live in a world that seeks to crucify the name of Jesus every day. In the same way the world had a good God before them in the person of Christ yet called him evil, we too live in a world that still calls good evil and evil good. Joseph's boldness didn't come in the form of him yelling at Pilate or fighting with the Sanhedrin. It came in the form of him showing up for Jesus when it mattered the most. How can God use our boldness to show up for him in a dying world that doesn't know him? To show up for him at a time when it matters the most? To show up for him when it might cost us something we cherish?

The other disciples eventually came around, but not until a resurrected Jesus literally walked through a locked door, appeared in front of them, and basically said, "Man, I told y'all this would happen. Why are y'all suddenly doubting me?" But Joseph's conviction allowed him to be bold before Jesus got his lick back and crucified death in his grave.

By the way, according to John, another Pharisee—Nicodemus—helped Joseph prepare Jesus' body for burial. Nicodemus had met with Jesus early in his ministry late at night, under cover of darkness, to talk with him, and like Joseph, he believed Jesus was the Messiah. He even spoke up for Jesus when the Temple guards threatened to arrest him (see John 7:50-51). And when Jesus died, John tells us that Nicodemus "came bringing a mixture of myrrh and aloes, about seventy-five pounds in weight" (John 19:39). But like Joseph, he was afraid to make his beliefs known. That's why you never want to opt out of sharing the gospel with anyone—even if they don't initially appear receptive. You never know.

So, the next time you have an opportunity to speak to somebody about how Jesus changed your life, and you find yourself worrying about what people might think or you're hesitant to speak because it's outside of your comfort zone, think of Joseph of Arimathea, and be bold.

Now, lest I close this book criticizing the disciples and giving props to a Pharisee, to be fair, the apostles did come to understand what it meant to be bold. In fact, I can't think of a better way to wrap things up than by talking about how they learned to be bold.

In one of the opening chapters of the book of Acts, Peter has just healed in Jesus' name a man who was crippled, and now he and John are out preaching the gospel when a group of priests and Sadducees come along and arrest them. Since it's already late in the day, they put them in jail to await trial in the morning.

Imagine what Peter and John might have been thinking. Jesus was just killed, and they are his followers. As I read about them, I can almost feel how fear must've curdled their courage all night as they awaited their fate in the morning. How their frantic hearts wouldn't let their exhausted eyes taste a sip of sleep. How creative their minds grew as they visualized the different ways they might be killed. Tired and terrified as fear caffeined their bodies awake, keeping them up all night with the moon. Sitting there, alone in the dark, as the prison walls grew in on them and began to swallow them whole. Remember, these were men who hid after Jesus was killed. So we should expect them to beg for their lives come morning.

The next morning, Annas, Caiaphas, and some other religious officials drag the likely frightened and sleep-deprived disciples in front of the high council and ask, "By what power or by what name did you do this?" (Acts 4:7). This is what we read next:

> Peter, filled with the Holy Spirit, said to them,
> "Rulers of the people and elders, if we are being
> examined today concerning a good deed done to
> a crippled man, by what means this man has been
> healed, let it be known to all of you and to all the
> people of Israel that by the name of Jesus Christ of
> Nazareth, whom you crucified, whom God raised
> from the dead—by him this man is standing before
> you well. This Jesus is the stone that was rejected by
> you, the builders, which has become the cornerstone.
> And there is salvation in no one else, for there is
> no other name under heaven given among men by
> which we must be saved."
> ACTS 4:8-12

Ladies and gentlemen, that's what I call a mic drop. This man sat up all night, with nothing but his thoughts and the devil's whispers to keep him company. Death was so near, he probably tasted it dancing on his tongue. And it's like he told himself, *If I'm going out, I'm going out like a G!*

The next thing the Bible tells us is that "the members of the council were amazed when they saw the boldness of Peter and John, for they could see that they were ordinary men with no special training in the Scriptures" (Acts 4:13, NLT). It says they also recognized Peter and John as having been with Jesus. So after conferring with one another, they let them go with the warning not to talk about Jesus anymore.

I don't know if they were shocked that they were let go. Maybe the boldness swelled inside of them and wouldn't let them care either way. But I do know they came right back at them with "Do you think God wants us to obey you rather than him? We cannot stop telling about everything we have seen and heard" (Acts 4:19-20, NLT). Where did this boldness come from? How did they become so reckless with their lives? Only God knew that day that the council wasn't going to kill them. So what created the roar in their chest? While sitting in prison with their innocent skin shackled, how did they become so free? Well, let me tell you.

That's the boldness you have when the Holy Spirit enters inside you and makes himself comfortable. When your body becomes a home for the living God, he does with it what he pleases. As soon as John and Peter were set free, they went back and told the others what happened, and they all "lifted their voices together" in prayer:

Sovereign Lord, who made the heaven and the earth
and the sea and everything in them, who through the
mouth of our father David, your servant, said by the
Holy Spirit,

"Why did the Gentiles rage,
    and the peoples plot in vain?
The kings of the earth set themselves,
    and the rulers were gathered together,
    against the Lord and against his Anointed"—

for truly in this city there were gathered together
against your holy servant Jesus, whom you anointed,
both Herod and Pontius Pilate, along with the Gentiles
and the peoples of Israel, to do whatever your hand
and your plan had predestined to take place. And
now, Lord, look upon their threats and grant to your
servants to continue to speak your word with all
boldness, while you stretch out your hand to heal, and
signs and wonders are performed through the name of
your holy servant Jesus.

ACTS 4:24-30

Do you see that? They're saying that there is nothing to
fear in Christ because nothing happens apart from God's will.
Even the evil that took place when Jesus was crucified was pre-
determined and directed by God. God was always in control.

Nothing happened by chance or because Herod, Pilate, or the Sanhedrin said so. God was orchestrating the whole thing from beginning to end.

And God is still sovereign. Nothing that happens today happens by chance. It is all according to his will. And so we should not be afraid to share our faith. We should not be afraid of losing our jobs for proclaiming that Christ is Lord. We should not be afraid of people at school or at work shunning us for proclaiming that Christ is Lord. We should not be afraid that people will think we're weird because we believe Christ is Lord. Because no matter what happens, God is going to use it all for his glory. He used Pontius Pilate, Herod, and the Pharisees, and if he used them, he's going to use you too.

Personally, I feel like a time is coming when God is going to make people choose between boldness or submission to the world. A time is coming when God's saints will be attacked for simply submitting to a higher authority than themselves. A time is coming when the world will try to make the church choose between boldness and passivity. They will tell us if we don't submit to what we feel, we are suppressing our true self and hurting the world around us. Don't believe that lie. Do not bend for a world that wants to break you. The same people who claim that they are "all accepting" contradict themselves when they reject the Christian worldview only because it goes against theirs. Respond to the contradiction with love, but be bold saints. Tell the truth now, because one day every lie will be lynched by the tongue, left to hang like dying fruit in the Mississippi heat. The mouth will no longer be a threat; it will only gossip about the glory of God.

Tell the truth now, because every jaw in heaven that did will be fixed with the sound of hallelujah, and everyone that swallowed the truth to live comfortably on earth will have no eternal peace. Tell the truth now because though this world hates truth, God still

TELL THE TRUTH NOW BECAUSE THOUGH THIS WORLD HATES TRUTH, GOD STILL HAS A PEOPLE OUT THERE WHO WILL HEAR AND RESPOND.

has a people out there who will hear and respond. He will use his people as instruments of truth to draw the most unlikely men and women to him. I believe in the last days, God will use his people to set the most rebellious souls free. If we remain faithful with God's truth, he will use us to soften the most hardened hearts. Angry fists will bloom into open palms of praise when we speak. Tell the truth now because, on the day Jesus returns to offer us heaven, we will be glad we did. On that day, the goose bumps on our skin will read the braille of glory in God's presence. Slander and persecution will remember our names no more, and we will sing with our whole bodies a right-now praise because we once gave the truth to a dying world.

Jesus has given us a command, and through his Holy Spirit, he has given us the power to carry it out. That's where our boldness comes from. As Paul says in Romans:

The Spirit helps us in our weakness. For we do not know what to pray for as we ought, but the Spirit himself intercedes for us with groanings too deep for words. And he who searches hearts knows what is the

mind of the Spirit, because the Spirit intercedes for
the saints according to the will of God. And we know
that for those who love God all things work together
for good, for those who are called according to his
purpose. . . . What then shall we say to these things?
If God is for us, who can be against us?

ROMANS 8:26-28, 31

Children of God, like our brother Paul said, we will never
go through purposeless evil. But if we are going to be faithful
evangelists, know that the world that called Christ a criminal
will come for us too. Yet even when it does, we can be confident that, as Paul writes, "neither death nor life, nor angels nor
rulers, nor things present nor things to come, nor powers, nor
height nor depth, nor anything else in all creation, will be able
to separate us from the love of God in Christ Jesus our Lord"
(Romans 8:38-39).

Who can be against us, indeed.

As believers in Jesus, we are all his disciples. Like Peter and
John, many of us are just ordinary people with no special training who happen to follow a man named Jesus—God in the
flesh who came to earth, worked mad miracles, healed the sick,
raised the dead, gave sight to the blind and hope to the hope-
less, and through his death and resurrection gave the gift of
life everlasting to all who believe in him. And that—and that

alone—gives us "the hope that we have," a reason to defend our faith. If we follow Jesus' example of speaking truth with "gentleness and respect," even if our words fall upon ears that don't want to hear, his will *will* be done.

So trust in the sovereignty of the Lord.

Be faithful.

Be obedient.

Be ready.

Be unapologetic in your presentation of the truth.

Honor him by honoring those around you—even those who disagree with you.

Remember, if you fail at times, that's okay. God can use everything.

And above all else—love people well.

Now go.

Tell the truth.

Be bold.

And win hearts.

NOTES

1. Paul David Washer, "Scandalous Gospel," Doctrine in Life, HeartCry Mission Society, July 23, 2018, https://heartcrymissionary.com/doctrine-in-life/scandalous-gospel.
2. John's references are from the Jehovah's Witness translation he used, the *New World Translation* (Patterson, NY: Watch Tower Bible and Tract Society of Pennsylvania, 2013).
3. Although in this case, the Jewish leaders were asking for the bodies to be removed early because of Passover—see John 19:31.

ABOUT THE AUTHOR

PRESTON PERRY is a poet, performance artist, teacher, and apologist from Chicago. Preston's writing and teaching has been featured on ministry platforms such as the Poets in Autumn Tour and Legacy Disciple. Preston is cohost of the popular podcast *With the Perrys*. He created Bold Apparel and the YouTube channel Apologetics with Preston Perry in order to engage the public in theological discourse. Preston and his wife, Jackie, reside in Atlanta with their four children: Eden, Autumn, Sage, and August.